Adirondack Wildguide

Michael G. DiNunzio

Adirondack Wildguide

*A Natural History of the
Adirondack Park*

Illustrations by Anne E. Lacy

Adirondack Wildguide is a joint project
of the Adirondack Conservancy
and The Adirondack Council.

Designed by Anne E. Lacy
Edited by Joseph Kastner
Set in type by Partners Composition
Utica, New York
Printed by Brodock Press, Inc.
Utica, New York

All illustrations and maps are
© Anne E. Lacy
with the exception of that on page 90.

Library of Congress Catalog Card Number
84-070873

ISBN 0-9613403-0-4 Hardcover

ISBN 0-9613403-1-2 Softcover

photo on opposite page: grass-pink
©Gary Randorf   1976

Production of the Adirondack Wildguide
was made possible largely through
the generosity of the estate of
Jean Wood Preston
for whom the Adirondacks were
a haven and a joy.

common mergansers fly overhead

Contents

Preface   9

Part 1   13

Land of the Barkeaters   15
Heritage of Stone   19
Gift of the Glaciers   23

Part 2   31
From Lakes to Lichens   33
introduction to Part 2

The Sun Lovers   35
    In the Shadow of Man   37
    Forgotten Fields   41
    Rise of the Phoenix   45
Trio of Giants   49
The Sand Dwellers   57
Wet Feet   67
    Flooded Forests   69
    Ponded Prairies   73
    Nature's Pickle Barrel   77
Realm of the Fishes   89
    Pools and Riffles   90
    Jewels in the Forest   95
Slopes of Evergreen   103
Islands in the Sky   113
Acknowledgments   127

Appendix   129

Checklists:
    Fish   130
    Amphibians and Reptiles   133
    Birds   134
    Mammals   138
    Trees   140
For Reading and Reference   143
Glossary   145
Index   150

looking south from the summit of Cascade

Preface

The fact is new and seems strange to many that there should be in the northeastern part of New York a wilderness almost unbroken and unexplored, embracing a territory considerably larger than the whole state of Massachusetts; a territory exhibiting every variety of soil, from the bold mountain that lifts its head up far beyond the limit of vegetable life to the most beautiful meadow land on which the eye ever rested.

REV. JOHN TODD, 1845
LONG LAKE

In many ways what the Reverend John Todd found new and strange when he visited the Adirondack region nearly 150 years ago will still seem new and strange to those who come upon it today.

The territory of which Todd spoke is no longer unbroken and unexplored but within the Adirondack Park true wilderness is still found beside hundreds of miles of paths and trails. Canoes glide silently along rivers little changed since early logging days—except that some are now wilder than before. Though the park is within a day's drive of millions of people and only a few hours from New York City, the unearthly cry of a loon can be heard piercing the silence of the back country. Untouched forests are mirrored in thousands of lonely lakes and ponds and from many mountain summits no sign of man is visible in any direction.

The park is a living storybook of the past, a representative sample of the elements that once made up the vast northern and eastern forests of the United States. Covering an area of more than 9,000 square miles in northernmost New York State, it is the largest

9

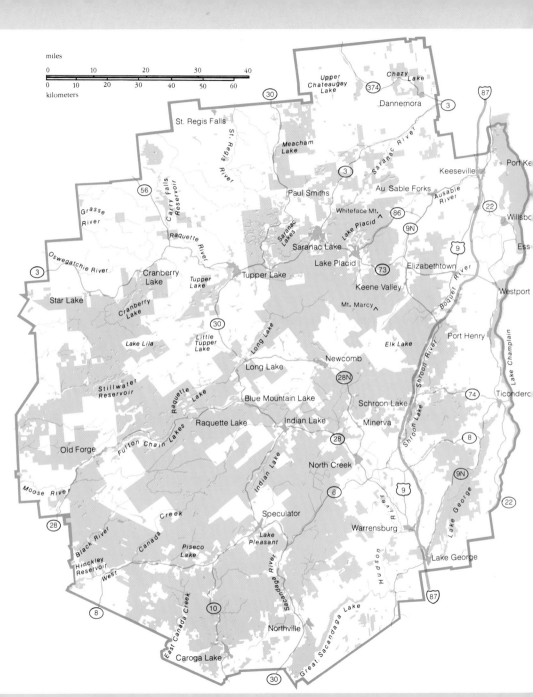

The Adirondack Park

Source: Adirondack Park Agency
Park Plan Map

state land

private land

park boundary

water body

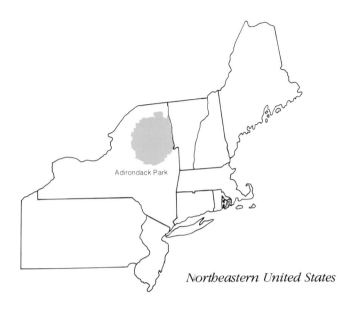

Northeastern United States

natural sanctuary in the nation—nearly three times the size of Yellowstone, our biggest national park outside Alaska. It is unique in being a curious blend of publicly owned State Forest Preserve (38%) and private holdings (62%) where thousands of people live and work year-round and thousands more vacation during all seasons.

This book has been designed to increase your enjoyment of the Adirondack Park by introducing you to some of the more common plants and animals of the region and to the natural communities in which they live. It presents an ecologist's view of the landscape that will help you interpret what you see and hear while traveling through the countryside and urge you to further exploration and adventure. The text and illustrations that follow will prove most useful when supplemented with various field guides—to trees, wildflowers, birds or mammals. A few of the best are included in the appendix.

To enjoy the park more fully, walk a short distance on one of the many marked state trails. Take in the damp woodland odors and listen to the flutelike song of a hermit thrush. The pines towering overhead cap a sinuous ridge of sand which marks the path of an ancient glacial riverbed. That litter of succulent shoots and grasses floating at the pond's edge are the leftovers from a muskrat's recent meal. Those ruffed grouse rocketing skyward on roaring wings were roosting in a stand of aspen that now fills the void left by wildfire nearly a generation ago.

Much of the park can be enjoyed from the window of a car or from a scenic overlook but beyond the cleared edges wild new worlds await your discovery.

Part 1

sunset from Haystack

Land of the Barkeaters

Tradition holds that the Iroquois Nation was founded by refugees who were forced to flee for their lives following an unsuccessful uprising against their oppressors, the Algonquins. Both groups originally lived along the shores of the St. Lawrence River in Canada but the Iroquois moved to central New York, leaving the North Country to the Algonquins with whom they continued an endless blood feud. According to legend the Iroquois referred to their northern neighbors as Ratirontacks (or Adirondacks), a term translated as "those who eat bark." Apparently this was a scornful allusion to the Algonquin's supposed lack of hunting ability which forced them to eat the inner bark of trees to keep from starving—a survival practice not uncommon among Indians of eastern North America.

Between these two nations lay a mountainous border country in which neither group settled, for its interior reaches were too inhospitable and daunting for anything more than infrequent hunting expeditions or for use as a hideout by traveling war parties. This no-man's-land remained unnamed by French and Englishmen alike. In 1837 Professor Ebenezer Emmons, appointed chief of the first natural history survey of the area, proposed that the mountains of the High Peaks district be called the Adirondack Group to commemorate the Algonquins who once hunted there. The name has since been used for the entire region.

The first European to record sighting the Adirondacks was Samuel de Champlain who, in 1609, traveled southward along the lake which now bears his name. For more than a century and a half the mountains were ignored by all but a few hunters, trappers, scouts and Indians. Logging, land clearing and battles took place on the fringes of the region but its interior remained virtually unexplored until shortly before the American Revolution when a group of speculators arranged to purchase more than a million acres from the Indians and the King of England. Settlement of this transaction was prevented by the outbreak of hostilities. After the war, ownership of Crown lands passed to the State of New York whose leaders lost little time initiating the process of selling the "Great Northern Wilderness" to private interests for pennies an acre.

By 1820 nearly all of the original public acreage in the Adirondacks had been conveyed to private owners. For the next half century, logging, lumbering, tanning and charcoal production proceeded at an ever-increasing pace. New York was the nation's leading timber producer in 1850, due in large part to harvesting within the Adirondacks. About this time degraded private lands began to revert to the state for unpaid taxes and through direct purchases at prices much higher than those paid for virgin forestland fifty years earlier. Large-scale destruction of Adirondack resources continued into the latter decades of the nineteenth century, aggravated by clear-cutting (removing entire forests) and the ravages of wildfires.

Public concern over the despoliation of the region led in 1885 to designation of the Adirondack Forest Preserve to protect state lands from further timber trespass and destruction by fire. In 1892 the legislature created the Adirondack Park, including both public Forest Preserve and private lands, chiefly for the purpose of defining the area within which future state purchases should be concentrated. Despite these efforts mismanagement of the Preserve continued and after a storm of protest New Yorkers ratified an 1894 constitutional amendment (now called Article XIV) which ensured that the Preserve "...shall be forever kept as wild forest lands." As a result of this action state holdings within the park cannot "be leased, sold or exchanged...nor shall the timber thereon be sold, removed or destroyed...." Since 1972 the Preserve has been managed by the New York State Department of Environmental Conservation under a State Land Master Plan, while development on private lands within the park has been placed under the authority of the Adirondack Park Agency.

The Adirondacks are perhaps best known for their high country, but elevations range from about 100 feet above sea level on Lake Champlain to the 5,344 foot summit of Mount Marcy, the state's highest peak. Forty-six mountains rise to 4,000 feet or above, and dozens of lesser ones create an impressive skyline, especially in the east-central portion of the park. Five major drainage basins funnel water from central highlands to lakes, reservoirs and river valleys at the periphery of the Adirondack area, including those

lumbering in the Adirondacks

feeding the St. Lawrence on the north, the Black River on the west, the Mohawk on the south and the Hudson and Lake Champlain systems on the east. Over 3,000 lakes and ponds are fed by tens of thousands of miles of brooks and streams. Mile after mile of piney woodlands shade the sands of ancient lakebeds while lush orchards line the fertile Champlain shores. Rolling evergreen forests of the lake and river country are flanked by sprawling wetlands below and hardwood hills above. Here bears still hole up in dens where Iroquois war parties slept and squirrels harvest acorns from oaks that Barkeaters might have seen as saplings.

Released from the icy grip of winter, a pool of snowmelt lies perched astride Cascade's barren ridge. ©Gary Randorf 197

Heritage of Stone

When seen in a photograph from space the Adirondacks look much like a monstrous mile-high turtle shell about 120 miles long by 80 miles wide, oriented in a northeast-southwest direction. This shell is actually the exposed top of an oval-shaped dome of rock whose roots plunge about nine miles into the earth, nearly halfway through the uppermost crust of the continent. A narrow neck of land in the Thousand Islands region of the St. Lawrence Valley forms the connecting link between Adirondack rocks and those of the Laurentian Shield of Canada to which they are related.

The process by which the Adirondacks were formed is ancient, complex and barely understood. About one billion years ago, when the earth itself was three and one-half billion years old, a shallow sea extended from northern Labrador to Georgia and westward into Mexico. Thousands of feet of sediments that had collected on the sea bottom were buckled and compressed by monstrous forces to a depth of about 15 miles. Here they were intruded by other minerals and subjected to intense pressure, heat and folding that slowly metamorphosed them into a mixture of various rocks.

The scarred face of Mount Colden rises majestically from the depths of Avalanche Pass in this view from Algonquin Peak. Storm waters running beneath the thin mantle of soil and vegetation have peeled huge patches of greenery from the bedrock.

Over a period of several hundred million years the Laurentian Shield, including the ancient Adirondack rock mass, was uplifted in a high plateau while at least 80,000 feet of overlying rock was eroded away. Seaward of this plateau a mountain rampart as high as the Himalayas stretched from Labrador to Alabama and west to Texas.

About 500 million years ago uplift had ceased and the region was eroded to a flat plain and flooded by a warm, shallow sea. It rose briefly above the waters, then was eroded and flooded once more. An episode of mountain building in what is now western New England caused erosional debris to wash over northern New York, capping the area with a layer of coastal plain rocks.

Hundreds of millions of years then passed without leaving a local record of geological events. Indirect evidence suggests that much of the northeastern United States remained above the sea during this lengthy period while insects, amphibians, trees and reptiles evolved, but it is doubtful that the region was mountainous.

The localized uplift that created the Adirondacks as we know them may have begun as recently as five million years ago, before modern man had evolved. Most of the sedimentary rocks that crowned the dome were stripped away, exposing the ancient metamorphic root zone we see today. Around the periphery of the dome, where uplift and thus erosion were less severe, many of the younger sedimentary rocks remain. A radial drainage pattern was established from which streams and rivers flow off the dome like spokes of a wheel. Giant rifts in the earth's crust, called faults or tension cracks, produced many of the northeast-trending valleys that characterize the region. Recent studies have shown that the Adirondacks are now rising approximately three millimeters per year at the center, three times faster than the Alps of Switzerland. We understand very little about this phenomenon, but it seems to be a temporary uplifting.

Rivers of ice coalesced and sloped northeastward to mile-high depths, forming the vanguard of continental glaciers. After the Big Ice had melted, localized mountain glaciers continued to disgorge their debris through upland valleys.

Gift of the Glaciers

While the basic shape and substance of the Adirondacks were formed by gigantic heavings and sinkings of the earth, the finishing touches were put on the landscape by the advance and retreat of several continental glaciers. Wherever you look you can see signs of glaciation—in the house-sized boulders that lie strewn over the countryside far from their points of origin, in the serpentine ridges of sand that wind across plains pocked by craters and dotted with low, oval mounds, and in the rock amphitheaters that scar mountainsides as if they had been gouged by a giant ice cream scoop.

Glaciation had little impact upon the underlying skeleton of bedrock, but the action of the ice produced major changes within local drainage systems and completely destroyed the existing soils. These effects were so profound they continue to exert a controlling influence over the park's plant and animal communities.

Between one and two million years ago a combination of celestial events led to sustained cooling of a few degrees Fahrenheit in the earth's climate. This resulted in more snow falling during the winter in Labrador and eastern Quebec than could

Sand, silt, clay and gravel carried by glacial ice were left behind when melting occurred. Some of this drift remained in piles of till, but meltwater flowing over and through the ice, as in the tunnel at left, sorted the debris into outwash.

melt during the short, cool summer. Snow and ice piled to heights of several thousand feet and pushed outward in all directions, advancing on the Adirondacks from the northeast. The upper surface of this mass was largely frozen, but its great weight caused the base to soften and it flowed over the ground like heavy tar, picking up rocks and boulders and scraping away the soil which had formed over hundreds of thousands of years.

At first shallow rivers of ice crept down valleys and around mountains, taking the path of least resistance. But as the ice coalesced and thickened, the highest summits were eventually engulfed and the surface of the land sank about 600 feet under the staggering load. As warmer periods alternated with cold over the span of a million years, four separate cycles of glacial advance and retreat occurred, each successive thrust of the ice sheets erasing all evidence of previous passages.

The last of the continental glaciers finally disappeared from the Adirondacks about 14,000 years ago. As the ice melted away from the St. Lawrence Valley, salt water rushed over the sunken landscape and flowed down the Champlain Basin, which became an arm of the sea. Gradually the earth rebounded sufficiently from its crushing burden to rise above sea level into the air once more. For another two thousand years or so isolated mountain glaciers remained on some of the peaks where perennial snow packs collected in hollows near summits and pumped ice into the flatlands below. These glaciers carved amphitheater-like cirques at the heads of mountain ravines and rounded valley walls into a U-shape by the grinding and polishing action of rock particles embedded in moving ice.

Glaciers altered the environment in two major ways. First, they wiped the slate clean, so to speak, by removing all soil and living material that stood in their path. Then, when glaciation ended, a veneer of clay, silt, sand and stone was deposited upon the bedrock. Accumulations of this glacial material blocked drainage systems, creating numerous lakes,

Mosses and polypody ferns cap a glacial erratic moved by the ice from some distant mountain to lie on the valley floor.

ponds and wetlands. Over the past 12,000 years new soils developed from raw minerals and organic matter.

As the ice sheets moved over the land they became charged with a jumbled assortment of boulders, rocks, pebbles, sand, silt and clay that is collectively called glacial drift. When the ice melted it did not bulldoze its way back northward, pushing debris before it, but simply dumped its load in place. In this manner the contours of the landscape were smoothed and rounded by the ice's deposits. Sometimes huge boulders called erratics were carried tens of miles by the ice and then left stranded like beached whales, mute reminders of the glacier's power.

Glacial drift which fell in an unsorted pile of material is known as till. Since the lower portions of the glaciers were loaded with the most material, the layer of till is thickest in the valleys and becomes progressively thinner, on the average, up the mountain slopes. Where melting water flowed over and through the drift it sorted out different materials in the process; lighter silts and clays were carried further downstream than heavier sands, stones and boulders. These water deposits are referred to as outwash and can be differentiated from till by several features.

Outwash is composed mainly of sand with various admixtures of stone and gravel. It is normally stratified, forming distinct layers, and its stones have been rounded by the tumbling action of running water. Till, on the other hand, is not sorted or stratified. Its stones are usually angled and it contains sizable amounts of silt and clay not found in the sandy outwash. Till occurs at all elevations up to about 4,200 feet, whereas outwash is limited to the level of postglacial streams and is therefore most common in valleys and along lakeshores.

Outwash deposits often create distinctive landforms such as eskers, kettles and kames, and you will find it relatively easy to recognize these sequels to the Ice Age. Eskers were formed when meltwater streams flowing beneath the ice in tunnels or at the bottom of crevasses caused gravel and sand to accumulate

Till is composed of an unsorted jumble of angular rocks and mineral debris of all shapes and sizes.

Outwash deposits are normally layered into beds of relatively homogeneous water-washed material, predominantly sands and rounded gravels.

27

Eskers, kames and kettles are common features on the outwash plains of the north-central Adirondacks. Circular kames stand where a hole in the ice filled with drift. Eskers follow the course of an ice tunnel. Their steep sides form a mound that often separates kettle ponds which lie in the depressions left by buried ice blocks.

aerial view of a kame, at left, and an esker separating two kettle ponds

kame

esker

within the narrow walls of their confines. As the ice melted these deposits were left as long, sinuous, steep-sided mounds that you can sometimes see running for miles across the land like giant mole tunnels.

Kettles formed in places where large blocks of ice became detached from the glacial front and were buried by outwash. When these blocks finally melted, the overlying outwash fell downward, creating pockmarks and hollow craters. Kettles range from tens of feet to nearly a mile in diameter. Where the bottom of a kettle hole lies below the water table a kettle pond can be seen.

Kames are roughly circular mounds of outwash that resulted when holes in the ice were filled with debris from streams flowing along the surface of a glacier. In places where debris filled the space between melting ice and a valley wall, a feature known as a kame terrace was formed.

The twelve thousand years or so which have passed since the last of the continental glaciers melted away has been a time of recovery and adjustment for the plant and animal communities of the Adirondack Park. Climatic changes during this period have fluctuated greatly in terms of average temperature and moisture conditions. The Adirondack climate of today is actually much cooler than that which prevailed for thousands of postglacial years.

Many plants and animals are still moving into the region for they have not had enough time to re-establish themselves since the ice left. Others exist only as relics of earlier times and are dying out. Lakes, ponds and wetlands are slowly disappearing as streams and rivers cut their way through the untold tons of drift that dam the impoundments. The park is a land in transition from which we can view the legacy of ice from our vantage point at a bend in the road of time.

Part 2

view of Lake Placid from the alpine community atop Whiteface Mountain

From Lakes to Lichens
an introduction to Part 2

At first the countryside of the Adirondack Park may appear as a random patchwork of forest, field, water and rock, of lowland lakes and mile-high mountain summits. But upon closer examination a sense of order will appear. There is a reason for everything. Those white birch trees have sprung from the ashes of yesteryear to clothe a fire-scarred mountain slope. That circle of tamaracks marking the onset of fall with a ring of smoky gold have grown around the edge of their favorite haunt, a woodland bog. Wherever similar conditions of soil, water and climate are found many of the same plants and animals live together as interacting communities.

Since most of the park has been disturbed by logging, fire, windstorm or agriculture, groups of "pioneer" species are common. They rush in to heal wounds on the landscape but are short-lived and soon give way to other communities that are better adapted to the new conditions.

There are several types of relatively stable, long-lived "climax" communities in the Adirondacks. Mixed-wood forests grow upon sandy glacial outwash soils, northern hardwood forests on the till soils of lower slopes, and boreal forests at elevations above approximately 2,500 feet. Alpine species dominate the arctic environment above timberline atop a dozen of our highest peaks.

Plants and animals specially adapted to watery environments are common in the park. Wetland communities are characterized by amphibious species that can tolerate soggy terrain and sites where flooding is normal during the growing season. Aquatic species live in the open-water communities of lakes, ponds, rivers and streams.

When trying to read the landscape start by examining a particular site. Is it partially flooded? Does it consist mainly of evergreens growing on a relatively flat, sandy surface? Are the woods filled with one or two species of young trees of the same age? The answers to these sorts of questions will be helpful when applying the information contained in the following chapters. Remember that these descriptions of our common natural communities represent a generalized classification scheme that is never duplicated exactly in nature.

paper birches spotlighted by the sun at Chapel Pond

The Sun Lovers

Open, sunlit spaces have always been part of the Adirondack environment, but the amount of this habitat has increased greatly since the coming of the white man. Specialized communities of plants and animals characterize these disturbed sites where grassy meadows, shrubby thickets and roadside clearings prevail.

There are many different communities of sun lovers, each adapted to life under different conditions of light, water, fertility and other factors. Some are composed of catastrophe species that follow in the path of wind, fire or intensive logging. Others are adapted to life with man or fill the fields he leaves behind. All are ephemeral features of the landscape. They flourish for a time, then give way as the forest closes in once more.

hayfield and High Peaks, Town of Essex

©Gary Randorf

In the Shadow of Man

Most of the Adirondacks remain wild and undeveloped but its villages, farms and roadways are an exception. These areas serve as habitats for diverse groups of species that thrive under conditions of continual farming, mowing, construction and other disturbance. Many of the plants and animals that live here are aliens, having been introduced from elsewhere. Few would survive for long if their habitats were allowed to revert to woodland. Relatively simple communities, like cornfields, lie alongside pastures and roadside ditches that often include complex assemblages of living things.

Farmlands are a good place to see some birds and mammals that are virtually restricted to plowed fields and open meadows. Flocks of rock doves flash in the sky, then seem to disappear as they pump along on pointed wings in the uncanny synchrony of close-order drill. Woodchucks shuffle through the grasses and take frequent breaks from grazing to sit upright with forepaws held like a begging dog. From here they survey the countryside for signs of predators which they promptly announce with a piercing whistle before diving for cover. The hawk spiraling overhead is most likely a red-tailed looking for movement from mice or snakes far below. Only when its fanned tail is backlighted by the sun does the telltale rufus glow appear.

A woodchuck surveys his domain from the jumbled foundation stones of an old homesite. The feather duster shape of the trees in the distance identifies them as American elms. Once the aristocrat of American shade trees, they are slowly dying from an introduced disease.

male bobolink in breeding plumage on an ox-eye daisy

eastern meadowlark with detail of tail

killdeer

Look for flashes of yellow, black and white that characterize a common trio of grassland birds. The eastern meadowlark sports a yellow breast accented by a broad, black, V-shaped necklace. In flight he alternates a rapid series of wingbeats with a short glide and looks brown with a white patch on either side of the tail. Two black bands across a white breast are the killdeer's trademark, as is his unmistakably loud and persistent call of "kill-deer,! kill-deer!" Male bobolinks look two-toned, having black undersides and white-dominated topsides. They often rise on fluttering wings and then drop like a falling leaf, exploding in song all the while. If he sits long enough you may catch a glimpse of the distinctive corn-yellow patch on the nape of his neck.

Old friends like dandelion, hawkweed, chicory and heal-all line the roadsides where members of the blackbird tribe are seen. Chunky little brown-headed cowbird males, which look all black from a distance, lack the long, keel-shaped tail of the grackle and the red-wing's showy epaulets.

An interesting newcomer to the park is the turkey vulture, which has expanded its range northward in recent years. It rocks back and forth on rigid wings that are held upward in the form of a "V" and is so large it is often mistaken for an eagle. Vultures can sometimes be seen near road-killed skunks, rabbits, raccoons and porcupines, but crows are the more common highway scavengers.

American crow

Disturbed in his afternoon nap, a coyote slips past a juniper. Grasses still maintain control of the abandoned field, but they are losing ground to an expanding clone of dogwood shrubbery (right), bushy white pines, aspen trees (right background), and cone-shaped eastern redcedars.

Forgotten Fields

Farming was never widespread in the Adirondacks and what little there was declined rapidly during the early years of this century. Many of the clearings once used for the production of hay, grain and pasturage for horses, dairy cattle and sheep are now abandoned and reverting to woodland. These old fields are filled with multilayered patchwork communities that are richer in animal and plant life than they were in the days of active agriculture.

Grasses, clovers, grains and "weedy" plants that came with man to the New World established themselves in our fields and meadows. They gained a foothold that now gives them a competitive advantage in the battle for existence that proceeds in the wake of the farmer, resulting in the maintenance of a relatively open habitat for several years following abandonment.

Thick sod helps prevent the germination of tree seeds. Rampant growth of established plants in early spring may kill new tree sprouts by shading them.

Within the soil, meadow grasses engage in a form of chemical warfare by secreting substances from their roots that inhibit the development of woodland species. Where livestock grazed for many years, plants which they found unpalatable, such as hawthorn, eastern redcedar and pasture juniper, abound.

During the early, grassy stage of plant succession small animals are plentiful. Insects such as grasshoppers and crickets help feed meadow jumping mice and short-tailed shrews, all of which may attract the attention of an American kestrel who hangs overhead on fluttering wings. Vesper sparrows flash their white outer tail feathers while American goldfinches sing "po-*ta*-to-chip" each time they fly to the top of their invisible roller coasters in the sky.

When cultivation, mowing and grazing are no longer practiced, grasses and herbs may dominate for a few years but woody-stemmed plants gradually assert themselves. Soon the fields are full of daisies, goldenrods, asters, St. Johnsworts, milkweed, teasel, mullein and pearly everlasting. Humpbacked clones of red-panicle dogwood and staghorn sumac appear and begin to expand. Aspens march from wooded borders into clearings where their roots send up shoots, creating a sloping thicket of progressively younger stems. White pine seedlings thrive here, becoming bushy in the sunlight. Hedgerows and shade trees add to the diversity of the community.

Scattered trees and shrubs attract bluebirds that sing their gurgling notes from perches near nest holes in rotting trees and fence posts. In brushy pastures look for a flash of the rich, deep blue color of indigo buntings whose rapid, strident singing comes forth in paired phrases sung in various pitches.

bull thistle   *American goldfinch*   *St. Johnswort*   *New England aster*

common mullein   common milkweed   chicory   goldenrod

(left)
White-tailed deer harvest the bounty from an aging orchard.

(right)
song sparrow beneath a blackberry bush

(far right)
Rocking on upheld wings, a turkey vulture floats above a lumber clearing. Quaking aspen (left) and pin cherry lead the invasion of forest trees that will soon shade out the tangle of brambles below.

Red fox, coyote, white-tailed deer and ruffed grouse feed within old orchards that herald the onset of fall with the pungent aroma of ripening fruit.

After two or three decades most old fields can no longer resist the forest invasion and they are dominated by pioneering trees. Since these species require full sunlight, however, their offspring are unable to grow in the shade cast by parent trees and their hour in the sun is virtually limited to a single generation. Thickets of pin cherry, aspen and white birch give way to red maple, white ash, elm and yellow birch, which are more tolerant of shading. Pin cherry begins to die out after about 30 years, trembling aspen after 40 to 60 years, and bigtooth aspen after 75 to 100 years. White birch may remain for 80 years or so while red maple and ash are likely to survive for another two or three decades. By this time a woodland community will have reasserted its claim over the long-forgotten meadowland.

Rise of the Phoenix

Within the past 100 years or so the primeval Adirondack forest was altered more drastically than at any time since the return of postglacial vegetation. Clear-cutting for charcoal and pulpwood became commonplace as logging and lumbering rose to a peak in 1905. During the late nineteenth and early twentieth centuries, wildfires raged in the wake of loggers who left vast quantities of highly combustible slash and bark on the forest floor. Thousands of acres of old-growth timber were destroyed during the "blowdown" of November, 1950 when a hurricane swept through the heart of the region. The stage was thus set for the development of communities that would rise from the ashes of destruction to heal and restore the land.

White pine stumps stand like gravestones on a sandy plain where wildfire followed the loggers half a century ago. Bracken fern, sheep sorrel and blueberries now share the task of restoring fertility to the soil.

When existing forest cover is entirely removed, site conditions are drastically altered. Sunlight floods the surface, causing great fluctuations in daily temperatures. Soil moisture which was pumped into the air by trees through their leaves is now available to other plants. Nutrients locked within litter on the forest floor are released to feed new growth. A number of sun-loving species are specially adapted to life under these conditions and they quickly move in to take advantage.

Buried seeds of trees and shrubs such as pin cherry, raspberry and elderberry awaken from a dormancy that may have lasted for a century or more. A flush of prickly briars usually covers the ground until thickets of saplings shade them out after about seven years. If hardwood stumps remain alive, vigorous sprouting occurs—particularly with red maple and beech. Where fire has killed trees and destroyed much of the soil's organic matter, light-seeded catastrophe species are blown in on the wind to fill the void. Aspens share this task with paper birch below about 2,500 feet, but only paper birch can thrive at higher elevations.

Openings on eskers and glacial outwash plains are favored sites for white pine unless a hot, deep-burning fire has severely damaged the sandy, infertile soil. After such a fire a heath-like community of blueberries, bracken fern, meadowsweet, clumps of grasses and patches of sheep sorrel may hold sway for many decades until trees are able to return. On some sandy plains along the eastern Adirondacks where wildfires were once a frequent occurrence,

forests of pitch pine have become established. This species can survive fires that destroy hardwood trees with which it competes for sunlight, thus capitalizing on adversity. It has the unusual ability to resprout at ground level if its trunk is killed or to sprout from the trunk and branches if a light fire burns its foliage away.

As successive plant communities develop on old burns, blowdowns and other disturbed sites, changing habitats are created that attract a variety of wildlife. During the early herbaceous stage of succession you can expect to see the streaked breasts of song sparrows as they flit in the undergrowth beneath chimney swifts that dart through the sky like cigars with sickle-shaped wings. Under the security of dense ground cover, red-backed voles scamper about in search of tender buds, roots, seeds and fruits. White-tailed deer come from the shadows of the woodland's edge to browse abundant sprouts and seedlings. Ruffed grouse are likely to be found here, as are black bears—especially during the berry season.

After shrubs and trees begin to shade out herbs and brambles, many animals of the earlier stage leave. Reduced visibility at eye level encourages you to rely more upon your hearing to locate wildlife. Listen now for the "sweet-sweet-sweet-sweeter-than-sweet" of a yellow warbler or the "pleased-pleased-pleased-ta-*meet*-ya" of a chestnut-sided warbler. If you are in the lowlands around the border of the park listen also for the persistent, squeaky chatter of a catbird that is sure to identify itself with a "meow" or two.

Early fall is a time of light and color in the hardwood forest.

Trio of Giants

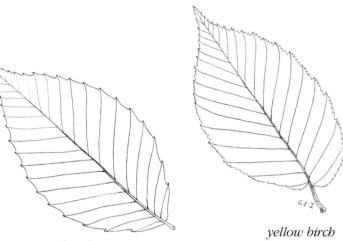

American beech

yellow birch

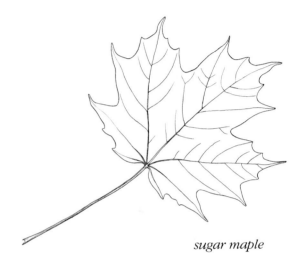

sugar maple

The most common plant and animal community in the Adirondack wilderness is the northern hardwood forest. It is an ever-changing world where the rustling green leaves of summer give way to the riotous colors of fall, where the pastels of spring relieve the barrenness of gray-brown branches clacking in the winter wind. Stand amid the hardwoods and look downward. A leafy carpet lies everywhere, a compost pile of nutrients and organic matter shed from above and recycled through decay to rise again in the trees. Remnants of the primeval hardwood forest remain but in most areas the community is a younger one that is still recovering from a century of exploitation.

Northern hardwoods grow best upon the deep, rich, glacial till soils of lower and middle-elevation slopes up to approximately 2,500 feet. Most plants would thrive on these sites except that few are able to reproduce under the deep shade cast by three ruling giants: American beech, yellow birch and sugar maple. For the most part any sun-loving pioneers such as quaking aspen and paper birch that are found here became established shortly after destruction of an earlier forest. As these pioneers gradually die away their place in the forest canopy is usually taken by one of the beech-birch-maple trio.

Black bears find beechnuts much to their liking and often leave tell-tale claw marks on trunks and a "nest" of broken twigs in the treetops where they have feasted.

Sugar maple is the dominant member of the northern hardwood community. In fact, the boundaries of the community can be defined by the presence or absence of this single tree. Unlike some of its associates sugar maple will grow only on soils that are well-drained, fertile and at least about two feet deep. Environmental conditions vary, of course, but where these requirements are met sugar maple reigns supreme. It is long-lived and covers the forest floor with seedlings that are more tolerant of shade than any other hardwood. As a particular stand matures toward a relatively stable climax condition, sugar maple tends to become more common throughout all levels of the community.

American beech is only slightly less shade-tolerant than sugar maple. Likewise, beech cannot grow in wet soils but it often leaves the community to venture onto the relatively infertile sands of glacial outwash deposits where sugar maple is unable to follow. In the past loggers were reluctant to cut beech since it is susceptible to internal rotting that is not evident until the tree is felled. After many cutting cycles in which

Eastern hemlock can be distinguished by a host of features in addition to the form of its leader. The dark blue-green foliage is arranged on flattened sprays that cast a dense shade beneath graceful, upturned boughs. Small, pendulous cones adorn the tips of branches and two white lines mark the underside of blunt needles which are attached to twigs by a slender stalk.

beech was left behind, the tree has become much more abundant than it was in the primeval forest. This superabundance has fostered the current epidemic of beech bark disease. A scale insect is host to the fungus that is decimating our mature beeches, but the old trees are prolific sprouters and they will no doubt produce a thicket of offspring from their roots.

Yellow birch is the tallest and most widespread Adirondack hardwood. Much less demanding of nutrients and drainage than beech or sugar maple, it is at home on a variety of sites from poorly-drained outwash to shallow upland tills. Although it is less shade-tolerant than either of its associates, yellow birch is an extremely aggressive species. It fulfills the role of a long-lived pioneer on small openings in the forest, especially on sites where mineral soil has been exposed. Once established this tree may live for 250 years or so, reaching over 100 feet into the air and measuring perhaps 4 feet in diameter. When scratched, its aromatic twigs exude an odor of wintergreen, making identification easy.

Far below the hardwood canopy, a striped maple shades the forest floor. Hobblebush arches above shining clubmoss, marginal woodfern and beech seedlings. Mosses cover rocks that rise above the litter of leaves.

An eastern chipmunk examines a beechnut bur while nestled among sprays of stair-step moss on a boulder.

Foamflower (left) and shining clubmoss (lower right) are common members of the community.

Many different trees, shrubs and wildflowers are scattered throughout the hardwood forest, each adapted to life within a slightly different habitat. Eastern hemlock favors cool, moist ravines and wetland edges where it betrays its presence from afar with a graceful curve at the very top that points away from the prevailing wind. Red spruce, highly prized by early loggers, is slowly regaining its stature as an important member of the community. Striped maple, diminutive and short-lived, is well-suited to life in the understory. If you aren't careful you may trip over a hobblebush for it has roots that weave in and out of the ground as though they weren't quite sure which way to go.

On the rich, leaf-covered humus of the forest floor look for the greenish-white flowers of wild sarsaparilla and the nodding, pale yellow blooms of bellwort. Spinulose woodfern is common here as are colonies of shining clubmoss that sometimes form "fairy rings" as new growth sprouts outside a circle of older, dying stems. Some of these rings may have descended from an individual plant that first grew here over a century ago. Since the ground is relatively dry and subjected to a heavy annual leaf-fall, mosses and liverworts are most common on elevated islands of rock, rotting logs, stumps and around tree bases where they are not buried in debris.

Camouflaged by its white winter coat, a snowshoe hare nibbles the tips of a hobblebush in the stark openness of mature hardwoods following a fresh snowfall.

Some areas within the hardwood community are particularly rich in nutrients and the most fertile sites can be found by looking for such trees as white ash, basswood, elm, and the shreddy-barked little eastern hophornbeam. Jack-in-the-pulpit, stinging nettle, foamflower and Canada violet are companions to the rich-site hardwoods and also serve as indicators of particularly fertile soils. In southern and eastern portions of the Adirondacks hardwoods like red and white oaks, shagbark hickory and butternut are found. If you look carefully you may even find remnant specimens of American chestnut, once the queen of American hardwoods, which was virtually eliminated from our forests by an exotic disease during the first half of the century.

Many species of animals are found within the diverse habitats of hardwood forests, but you may have trouble seeing them through the dense cover. Listen for the hoarse, buzzy, robinlike song of the scarlet tanager and the crescendo of the ovenbird's "teacher-TEAcher-TEACHER." The presence of a broad-winged hawk is often announced by the resonant "tuck-tuck-tuck" of an alert chipmunk who feels obliged to pass the word long after all danger has passed. As you inspect tender hardwood shoots for the angled knife-cut of a snowshoe hare or the mashed stub left by a browsing white-tailed deer, try to make out the hesitating, question-and-answer monotony of the red-eyed vireo's chant.

Each year in early spring there comes a time when hobblebush has its day, a fleeting moment poised between winter gray and summer green.

photo by Eliot Porter
courtesy of
The Adirondack Museum

Autumn sunlight brightens a bend in a road winding through mixed woods.

The Sand Dwellers

red maple

A dark forest of conifers flanks a meandering stream. White pines crown a low mound rising from a boggy mire. Ferns and mosses form a greensward beneath a mosaic of needles and leaves. These are the mixed-woods, a subtle blend of communities that occur wherever glacial meltwaters flowed over the landscape, leaving deposits of outwash behind.

Mixed-woods are common throughout the Adirondacks for the region is rich in outwash. Rivers gushed miles-wide from the melting ice, choked beyond capacity with a load of mineral debris that quickly filled entire valleys with up to several hundred feet of material. Over the past 12,000 years streams cut through much of this glacial drift, leaving the ancient riverbeds and floodplains as raised platforms of sand.

Living conditions on sandy, glacial outwash are more harsh than those on soils derived from glacial till. This favors the development of communities consisting primarily of evergreens with varying amounts of certain hardwoods. Nutrient-rich silts and clays are in short supply here, creating a general lack of fertility that precludes establishment of a northern hardwood community.

Eastern white pines can be identified from a great distance since they commonly rise far above their neighbors in the forest canopy.

A bed of needles covers the steep slope of an esker beneath towering white pines.

Sand does not hold moisture well, so precipitation percolates quickly through upper levels until it reaches the water table. If ground water is normally more than about four feet below the surface, as it is on eskers and kames, droughty conditions are common during dry summer months. Young plants often have difficulty establishing a deep enough root system to avoid desiccation and fires are more likely to occur in such areas.

On many sites a cementlike hardpan layer lies between one and two feet below the surface. It causes shallow rooting of trees which makes them susceptible to wind-throw during severe storms and also limits the availability of nutrients. When rainfall is heavy, water may sit atop the hardpan and drown roots, but in drier times plants are effectively sealed off from the moisture underlying the pan.

*starlit silhouettes of eastern white pine (left) and
red pine*

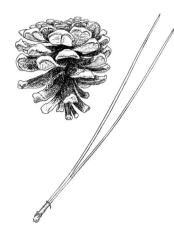

red pine

*needles in twos;
short, roundish cones*

Major tree species of mixed-wood forests include red spruce, balsam fir, hemlock, red maple, black cherry and the ubiquitous yellow birch. Hemlock and its hardwood associates dominate on richer pockets of outwash soil where scrubby specimens of American beech are also found. On sites where the water table rises to within about three feet of the surface the percentage of spruce and fir increases. Well-drained sandy knolls and terraces are sometimes capped with pure stands of red or white pine, both of which are very drought-resistant. White pine, which is scattered throughout the community, can be identified from a great distance because it commonly rises 50 to 60 feet above the surrounding forest. Along the eastern edge of the park extensive pine forests cover outwash plains and old glacial lakeshores. Pitch pine is common here on particularly sterile soils.

eastern white pine

*needles in groups of five;
long cones*

plants of the mixed-wood forest floor

1. *moss and lichens on tree trunk*
2. *red maple seedling*
3. *balsam fir seedling*
4. *blueberry*
5. *bluebead lily*
6. *starflower*
7. *Canada mayflower*
8. *twinflower*
9. *bunchberry*
10. *goldthread*

*a melange of leaves from
the edge of the mixed woods*

©Gary Randorf 1977

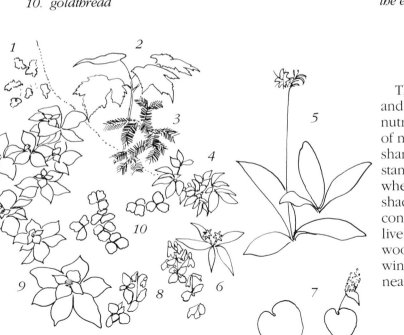

The forest floor in mature mixed-woods is damp and acidic, slowing the rates of decomposition and nutrient cycling. This promotes a thick accumulation of needles and spongy organic material that contrasts sharply with the leaf litter found under hardwood stands. Blueberries and sheep laurel grow in patches where rays of filtered sunlight penetrate the deep shade of conifers. Ground cover is virtually continuous, with a profusion of mosses and liverworts carpeting logs and boulders. Spinulose woodfern, Canada mayflower, wood sorrel, wintergreen and dwarf dogwood seem to grow nearly everywhere.

c.c.l.

63

common birds of the mixed woods

1. *red-breasted nuthatch*
2. *golden-crowned kinglet*
3. *ruby-crowned kinglet*
4. *black-capped chickadee*
5. *pine siskin*
6. *evening grosbeak*
7. *downy woodpecker*

Roving bands of golden-crowned kinglets, evening grosbeaks and pine siskins can be heard singing and calling to each other among the branches of evergreens where they search for seeds, buds and insects. If you stop to inspect a midden-heap of cone scales lying upon a mossy log or at the base of a tree be prepared for the scolding chatter of a red squirrel who finds your presence a threat to his feeding territory. With the help of binoculars you may be able to catch fleeting views of many different species of warblers, the colorful "butterflies of the bird world."

red crossbill in a red pine

misty afternoon on the Grass River Flow

Wet Feet

Wetlands are plentiful here in the Adirondacks, covering about 900,000 acres (15%) of the park's wildlands. There are three basic types: bogs, swamps and marshes. Trees and shrubs grow in swamps, floating-leaved and grass-like plants in marshes, and peat mosses grow alongside shrubby heath plants in bogs.

Wetlands can form virtually anywhere, the only criterion being that water must lie at, or very near, the surface of the ground during at least a portion of each growing season. They are most numerous in the shallow depressions of outwash plains and are rare on sloping terrain. But don't rely upon the presence of water to identify a wetland community. Many of them appear to be quite dry throughout much of the year and it is normal for some to lack surface water except during spring.

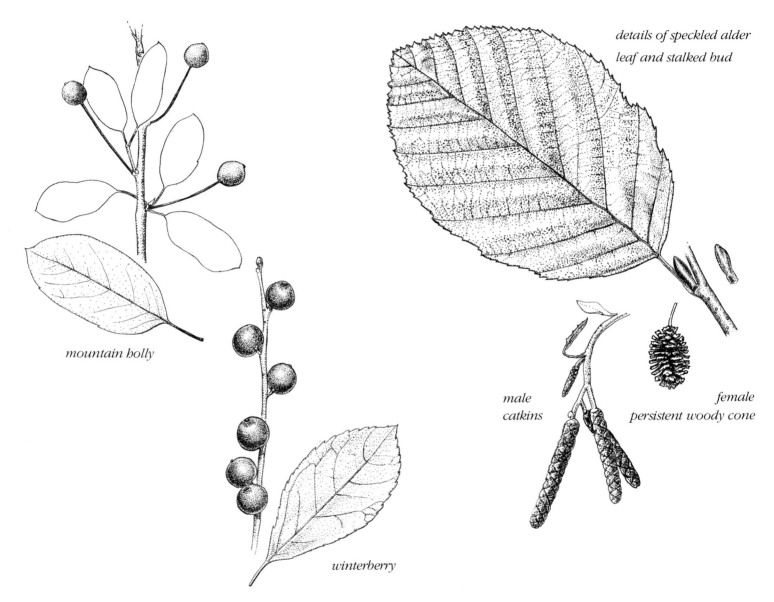

details of speckled alder leaf and stalked bud

mountain holly

winterberry

male catkins

female persistent woody cone

Flooded Forests

Swamps account for more than 95% of the wetland habitat within the park. They are the least wet of our wetlands since flooding of the surface is often restricted to the spring and for short periods following heavy rains. In many swamps standing water may not be visible at the surface during dry years but saturation of the soil prevents the growth of a less water-tolerant community.

Shrub swamps are normally found in areas that are flooded too long and too deeply for trees to tolerate, for example, around the margins of ponds and bogs where the water may reach depths of six inches or more. Shrubs can survive in these conditions and since they are resistant to moderate ice scouring and damage from flowing water, they are also common in low-lying river floodplains and along streams. Buttonbush, willows, various dogwoods, speckled alder, winterberry, wild raisin, sweet gale and mountain holly are typical members of shrub swamp communities.

The limited depth and duration of flooding in wooded swamps permits trees to grow here. Since trees cannot root deeply in wet soil, they are susceptible to wind-throw. For this reason wooded swamps often contain a jumble of upturned roots and fallen trunks that create a hummocky terrain where mossy, fern-covered mounds alternate with water-filled pits. Typical swamp trees include red maple, black ash, balsam fir and black spruce. Northern white cedar may also be present but it is a favorite food of white-tailed deer, and in areas having a large deer population few young trees survive long enough

Speckled alders choke the floodplain of a meandering stream.

69

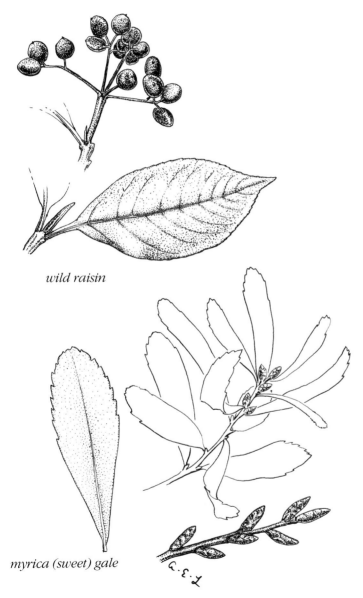

wild raisin

myrica (sweet) gale

to grow beyond the "browse line" about five feet from the ground. Larch (tamarack) grows well here, usually on soils that are waterlogged throughout the entire growing season. The larch is our only deciduous conifer, losing its needles after they turn a distinctive golden-brown color in the late fall.

Deciduous wooded swamps are mostly found along the periphery of the park where wet soils that are particularly rich in nutrients provide a habitat for American elm and silver maple. In the central Adirondacks prolonged cold temperatures cause a short growing season favoring wet-site conifers which are more hardy and less demanding of nutrients.

During the drier months of summer and fall, swamplands filled with coniferous trees are sometimes confused with a type of moist, mixed-wood community called a "spruce flat." The difference can be seen easily, even where spruces and firs are common in each community. Conifer swamps are distinguished by a luxuriant green carpet of sphagnum (peat) moss covering dark humus-rich muck. Spruce flats have a deep layer of needles—and little else—lying on the forest floor atop mineral soil.

Birdlife within shrub and deciduous wooded swamps includes a number of wetland specialists such as the swamp sparrow, alder flycatcher, American woodcock and wood duck. Coniferous wooded swamps attract many of the same species found in other evergreen forests, such as ruby-crowned kinglets, both red-winged and white-winged crossbills, Canada warbler, magnolia warbler and purple finch. In cold, high-country swamps look for the northern waterthrush and listen for the weak, wheezy, "chick-che-day-day" of the boreal chickadee.

Sphagnum moss forms a bright golden-green carpet beneath the conifers in a spruce swamp.

*Moving slowly between statuesque poses, a great
blue heron patiently hunts the shallows of a
cattail marsh. A northern harrier patrols
overhead while a spread-winged damselfly takes
a brief respite on the leaf of a pickerelweed.*

Ponded Prairies

Marshes are the wettest of our wetlands. They occur
where the soil is waterlogged throughout the
growing season and is normally flooded to depths
ranging from a few inches to about six feet.
Regardless of the depth or duration of flooding,
marshes are essentially wet prairies covered by
grasses, sedges, reeds, and other plants whose
combined effect reminds one of partially-submerged
grassland. The community is most common along the
margins of lakes and ponds, although it may be found
interspersed among other types of wetland or in
slow-running backwater reaches and oxbows of rivers
and streams.

In places where water floods the surface for only a
short time and the upper few inches of soil may dry
out a bit during the growing season, a form of marsh
called wet meadow may occur. Wet meadows rapidly
invade drained, abandoned beaver ponds. They also
flank river flood plains where the ice floes of spring
are massive enough to scour away any woody plants
that may take root. Clumps and tussocks of coarse
grasses, sedges and herbs such as loosestrife, vervain,
dock and smartweed stand on low pedestals of
organic matter in the air above the soggy soil.

Prolonged, shallow flooding creates a habitat
where cattails, rushes, bur-reed, arrowheads and
pickerelweed sink their roots and rhizomes deep into
the muck to help them withstand the ceaseless tugs
and jostles of wind and wave. As water depth
increases so does the relative occurrence of
pondweeds, waterweeds, coontails and water lilies.
They make no effort at maintaining a rigid posture
and float like anchored islets, with only the upper
surfaces of their leaves exposed to the atmosphere. At
depths exceeding about three feet plants have
difficulty growing above the surface of the water
and marshland merges into the open-water
community beyond.

Marshes are highly productive, for they make
efficient use of the energy in sunlight to drive the
chemical machinery that transforms soil, air and
water into leaf, fin, fur and feather. Nutrients washed
from uplands enrich marsh waters and become
incorporated within oozy sediments that are in turn
stabilized by fibrous root mats. Moving water
provides an ample supply of oxygen so that the cycle
of growth and decay proceeds uninterrupted.

Several herbivores graze our wetland prairies,
including such diverse animals as insects, snails and
muskrats. Most numerous of all are the microscopic
free-floating zooplankton which feed within the green
clouds and slimy strands of algae that crowd stems
and other debris of the shallows. Fish feed upon
plankton, plants and insect larvae and in turn may
become food for osprey, herons or even man.

Spring brings a symphony of sound to the marsh.
Even while ice and snow remain, red-winged
blackbirds shout "conk-a-rees" from atop swaying
reeds and cattails. Wood frogs awaken from their
winter slumber to celebrate ice-out with a peculiar

water-l

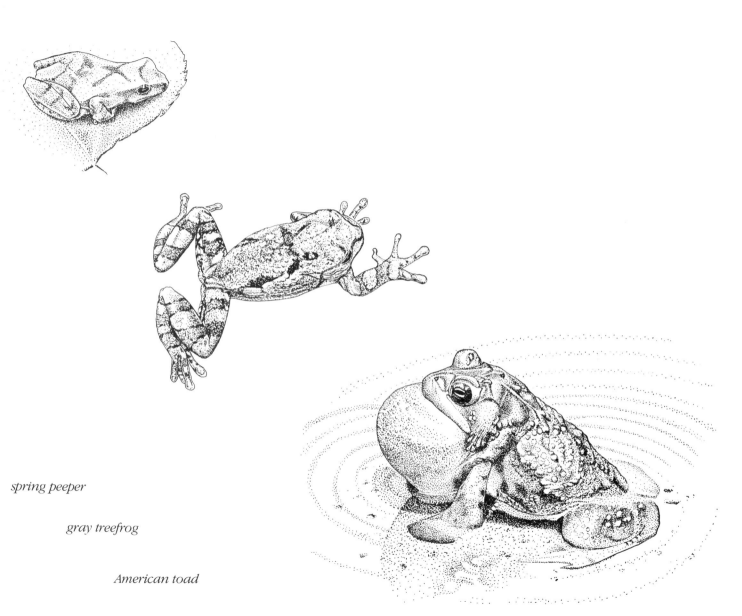

spring peeper

gray treefrog

American toad

75

ducklike clacking. Soon the chorus is joined by the strident calls of tiny spring peepers and the short trills of gray treefrogs.

As spring passes into summer, green frogs serenade at dawn with a deep banjo-like "plunk." Listen carefully and you will very likely hear the distinctive "witchity-witchity-witchity-witch" of the colorful common yellowthroat. The most peculiar sounds likely to emanate from the shallow water of cattail beds or sedgy meadows are made by the American bittern. Called "stake driver" and "thunder pumper," the bird makes two interesting noises. One sounds like the loud "thwack" of a hammer driving a wooden stake while the other is reminiscent of the low, hollow sucking sound of an old wooden hand pump.

Here and there within the marsh, looking like scattered lawn clippings, short stems and leaves of water plants float on the surface or are washed ashore. These are the remains of material gathered for food by a muskrat. A mound of matted vegetation rising from one to several feet above the water marks the muskrat's home, which lacks the large sticks and distinctively-gnawed branches of the more substantial beaver lodge. In winter smaller mounds of vegetation, called push-ups, form snow-covered igloos inside which muskrats can feed in safety at the surface. The insulating effect of this plant material tends to keep a hole open in the ice through which the "rat" can come and go at will. Sooner or later the muskrat falls prey to a coyote, owl, fox, hawk or even a mink. All are part of the complex web of plants, animals, nutrients and energy that bind the marsh into a cohesive, interdependent unit.

Swaying in rhythm with the wind-blown sedges, arrowheads and marsh ferns, an American bittern guards her nest.

Nature's Pickle Barrel

Bogs have long been looked on as places of myth and
mystery, the haunts of strange, unearthly creatures
where eerie perils await the unwary stranger.
Common sense may dispel these ideas, but the bog
remains a fascinating, topsy-turvy world where it is
possible to walk on water, watch plants eat animals
and reach through a dark window into the past.

*A North Country bog glows in the yellow light of
an October afternoon. Leatherleaf is the bronze-
colored shrub scattered throughout, with sheep
laurel (drooping leaves) and bog rosemary in
the foreground. Two black spruces seem to peer
across a pool of open water toward the smoky-
gold tamaracks (larch) on the far shore.*

77

©Gary Randorf 1974

Pitcher-plants hold their water-filled leaves above a sphagnum bed. Insects attracted to the plants cannot crawl upward against the hairs which line the vase and they drown, giving up their nutrients to the vegetation.

In the Adirondacks, bogs commonly form in shallow lakes, ponds or wet depressions having little inflow or outlfow of water. Lack of drainage leads to the accumulation of waterlogged, partially-decomposed organic debris called peat. As more and more matter accumulates the bog basin slowly fills. Peat deposits release weak acids into the water and it becomes saturated with various compounds that impart a characteristic tea-colored stain. Sunlight is unable to penetrate as deeply as before, and this reduces the ability of submerged green plants to enrich the bog with oxygen.

Bacteria and fungi, which are the principal decomposers of organic material, operate most efficiently in warm, moist (not wet) oxygen-rich environments. Breakdown of dead organisms into simpler compounds and elements is hindered by the cool climate, excessive wetness and lack of oxygen in bogs. The cycle of growth and decay that typifies other types of wetlands eventually slows to a virtual standstill.

Sphagnum moss, sedges and low shrubs gain a foothold and spread rapidly. Gradually the moss and other plants thicken into a living carpet that partially engulfs woody stems, grassy clumps and floating leaves of buckbean. A tangled mass of stems, leaves and roots grows slowly outward from the bog's edge and blankets the pond, sealing its depths from light and oxygen. This causes more and more acids to accumulate in the water.

Once the bog becomes strongly acidified a curious phenomenon takes place. Plants find this water difficult to absorb in much the same way as animals have difficulty drinking salty liquids. Under these conditions two qualities are favored: ability to conserve precious water reserves and adaptation to low nutrient levels.

Members of the heath family such as bog laurel, Labrador tea, leatherleaf, bog rosemary and cranberry are well suited to bog life for they have leaves which retard evaporation through such adaptations as waxy coatings, rolled edges and fuzzy undersides. Pitcher plants and sundews are also found here for they have evolved simple yet effective insect-trapping devices that digest their victims and provide the plants with nitrogen, a nutrient that is otherwise in very limited supply. Delicate wildflowers such as grass pink and white-fringed orchis hold a surprise: they are growing here far from the land of their evolutionary origins in a habitat that features many of the acid, infertile conditions typical of jungle environments.

Journeying across the surface of a bog is much like walking on a water bed for the mat often floats above an open pool and is little more than an amorphous mass in which one slowly sinks until a new state of equilibrium is reached. Dead plant material falls from the mat like a fine rain, filling the pool with peat. Once this organic matter leaves the shallow layer of oxygenated water near the surface it undergoes little, if any, decomposition.

For the most part bog water contains large numbers of a few acid-tolerant species of microscopic animals and blue-green algae. Several insects spend at least part of their life cycle in bogs but most are only

a young mink frog on round-leaved sundews

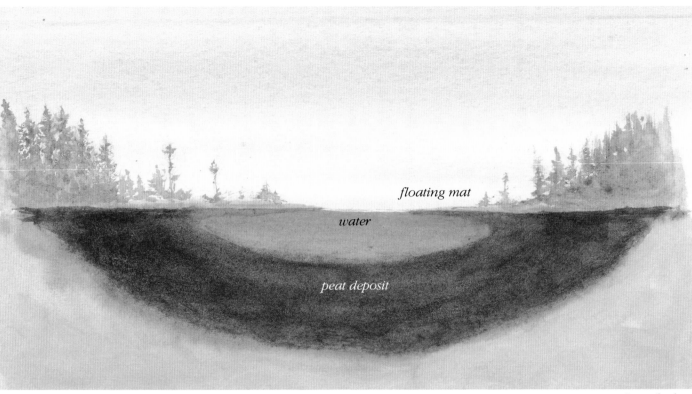

floating mat

water

peat deposit

cross section of a bog

plants of the bog community

1. *leatherleaf*
2. *bog rosemary*
3. *cottongrass*
4. *sheep laurel*
5. *bog laurel*
6. *Labrador tea*
7. *sphagnum mosses*

black-backed woodpecker

visitors. Frogs take advantage of this insect life and in turn may become prey for a northern harrier or an American kestrel. Many Adirondack specialties can be found here, including black-backed and three-toed woodpeckers, spruce grouse, Lincoln's sparrow, olive-sided flycatcher, rusty blackbird and the curious little bog lemming. You may be fortunate enough to receive an inquisitive visit from a family of gray jays—northern counterparts of the more familiar blue jay—whose repertoire of muted calls befits their ghostly flight.

The bog is a tomb of history. Bodies of long-extinct beasts such as the mastodon, mammoth and ground sloth have been found preserved in their darkness (though not within the park), trapped and suffocated in the prehistoric muck. All bogs are richly endowed with the identifiable remains of plants, including pollen from trees and wildflowers growing in the general region. Since each kind of plant sheds a distinctive form of pollen, scientists can inspect various layers of peat and determine the nature of the vegetation in and around the bog at different times since the last glaciation. From this information basic climatic data can be deduced. Our cool, moist climate that favors the growth of spruce and fir represents a recent return to conditions reminiscent of early-postglacial times. Intervening climates were generally warmer; the relatively dry periods favored the growth of pine, and the moist periods favored hemlock.

A male spruce grouse displays his breeding plumage from the branches of a tamarack.

black spruce

pendant cones with ragged scales;
sharp, persistent needles borne on woody pegs

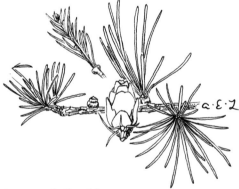

tamarack (larch)

upright cones; deciduous needles in whorls on
short, woody spur shoots

As a bog pond fills with peat on the bottom and an ever-thickening mat of sodden vegetation on the surface, it becomes more and more like a swamp. Larch and black spruce grow on the mat wherever their seedlings can gain a foothold. Establishing a seedling is one thing but supporting a large tree is quite another and the unstable peat causes many of the shallow-rooted invaders to topple before wind and under snow. A general climatic warming trend lasting several years may cause the surface of the mat to dry out a bit. This promotes increased oxygenation, decomposition and nutrient availability, all of which encourage tree growth. Over the thousands of years that pass as bogs develop and mature several waves of trees may advance and retreat. Poke a long stick through the mat in a treeless area and you may find old logs and stumps, some of them charred by ancient wildfires.

Some bogs eventually become forested. Increasing numbers of trees and shrubs suck water from the sphagnum and pump moisture into the air. Since drying and shade help destroy the sun-loving plants of the bog mat, the process of forestation is accelerated as nutrients are set free by decay to nourish more woody growth.

Tamaracks flank a black spruce clone on the
quaking mat overhanging a bog pond. Young
spruces develop from rootings made when the
lower branches of a parent tree are buried in
moist sphagnum.

No longer supported by living roots, a tamarack falls slowly across a moonbeam into the depths of the bog.

A few bogs collect so much peat that they develop a raised, dome-shaped center causing water and nutrients to drain away to the rim. Inputs of nutrients are then limited to those that are dissolved in rain and snow or that drift in as dust particles. Eventually a state of dynamic equilibrium is reached in which the mat cannot rise any higher due to its inability to accumulate water, which is pulled downslope by the force of gravity.

Myths are often based on fact and those associated with bogs are no exception. After all, these are places where strange beasts lie deep within a watery grave, vegetation floats on a desert island in a tea-stained acid sea, carnivorous plants mock traditional roles of hunter and hunted and wanderers from the lush tropics find a home among immigrants from the land of the midnight sun.

An inquisitive gray jay perches momentarily on a dead tree.

A male brook trout in breeding colors defends his pool in a mountain stream.

Realm of the Fishes

Swift-flowing rivers and streams have characterized the Adirondacks for millions of years but lakes and ponds are much more recent additions to the landscape. Together these aquatic communities form one of the region's great attractions. Within the park some 30,000 miles of brooks and streams feed 1,000 miles of rivers and nearly 3,000 lakes and ponds.

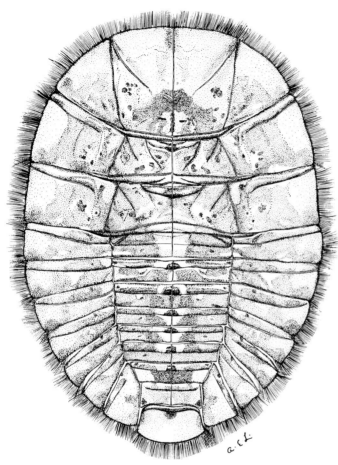

*larval form of a water-penny beetle
(actual size about 1/4 inch)*

by Anne E. Lacy
courtesy of the Smithsonian Institution

Pools and Riffles

Water away from the sea seems duty-bound to return home as quickly as possible, although many obstacles lie in wait including sidetrips through the bodies of plants and animals or detention within subterranean aquifers. A large portion of the total amount of precipitation is drawn into the air by the sun, either directly or through living plants. But much of the moisture that remains on the ground seeps through shallow soil until it enters waterways flowing over the land.

In headwater regions streams are relatively clear, cold, oxygen-rich and nutrient-poor. They flow quickly over numerous falls, rapids and cascades, cutting V-shaped beds along steep paths through glacial overburden and into the underlying bedrock by the abrasive action of eroded material. Few algae are attached to the boulders and large rocks in these streambeds and rooted aquatic plants are scarce.

Fast streams consist of a series of turbulent riffles alternating with quiet pools. Riffles are regions of food production where plants such as algae and water mosses use the energy of sunlight to transform carbon, hydrogen, oxygen and mineral nutrients into sugars, starches and living tissue. Food and oxygen are plentiful here, creating a habitat suitable for a variety of aquatic species including black-fly larvae, nymphs of mayflies and caddisflies, water pennies

ite-water riffles mark the end of a pool on the West Branch of the Ausable River.

©Gary Randorf 1975

and hellgrammites. This is also the home of our highly-prized native brook (speckled) trout and several lesser-known fish species like the blacknose dace, fathead minnow, rosyface shiner and greenside darter, all of which move freely between riffles and pools.

Living organisms and organic debris from riffles continually move downstream and collect in pools where decomposition takes place. Riffle-dwellers that are carried here often suffocate since lessened flow rates in these areas may fail to move sufficient oxygen over their respiratory organs. Nymphs of dragonflies and damselflies are adapted to this environment, as are water striders and water boatmen. Decomposition within pools recharges the water with carbon dioxide and nutrients which are utilized by organisms living in downstream riffle reaches.

As brooks gather into wider, deeper streams and rivers in less mountainous terrain they slow their pace, begin to meander and take on more and more of the characteristics associated with standing water.

Increased amounts of dissolved substances add color and suspended particles make waterways more turbid. As the darkened water slows and meanders in the sunshine it begins to warm and this produces important secondary effects. The rate of decomposition increases as the temperature rises, consuming more oxygen in the process. But oxygen is replaced at fewer and fewer intervals as turbulent riffles (which function as aerators) give way to smooth-flowing runs. Warm water cannot hold as much oxygen as cold water can, so the availability of this precious gas may drop to such a low level that insects, fish and other aquatic animals have difficulty surviving within the altered environment.

At this point, the flowing water community blends into an assortment of plants and animals characteristic of marshes or, if the water is deep enough, of lakes and ponds. Vegetation clings to the rocks and gravel of these streambeds and rooted plants become common in the silt and mud that accumulates wherever the current slackens.

reflections in a rocky pool

photo by Eliot Porter
courtesy of The Adirondack Museum

Its waters locked under ice and a blanket of snow, the St. Regis Canoe Area stretches for miles beneath the mountain for which it was named.

Jewels in the Forest

Open water contrasts sharply with the dense forestlands of the park through all seasons of the year. On bright, sunny days ponds and lakes sparkle like diamonds strung on the shimmering liquid threads of their funneling inlet streams and solitary outlets. When skies are somber they reflect this mood also, for they are the mirrors of the heavens. In the starkness of winter neither ice nor snow are able to disguise the locations of these water bodies. For several months they stand alone as flat, unvegetated expanses, lacking the muted hues of the slumbering conifers and leafless hardwoods that outline their shorelines more sharply than before.

Lakes and ponds are evanescent features of the landscape that appear in a flash of geologic time and then quickly disappear. Since most of our ponded waters are relics from the age of glaciation they are no more than about 10,000 years old.

In the first few hundreds of years following the melting of the "Big Ice" large segments of valleys and lowlands were submerged to considerable depths due to blockage of drainage basins by till and outwash. Huge ice blocks lay buried in this drift and slowly melted, forming kettle holes that often filled with water. Shallow lakes and ponds were numerous. It was a land of raw sand, gravel, boulders, bedrock and moisture. Over the past ten millenia streams that drained these postglacial water bodies gradually cut their way through the drift and breached many of the ancient impoundments. This has resulted in a marked lowering of general water levels and a segmentation of once-large lakes into strings of smaller basins connected by flowing water.

After thousands of years of weathering, erosion, silting and revegetation most of the park's endowment of open water has vanished, leaving a wealth of wetlands, meandering streams and dry lakebeds. Nonetheless, there are still over 50 large lakes and reservoirs with at least one square mile of surface area, about 2,700 smaller lakes and ponds and a multitude of ecologically important water bodies that are too small to have received names or to be mapped as permanent open water.

Lakes move in rhythm with the cycle of the seasons just as all natural communities do. During winter and summer most of our lakes are layered into two major zones with lighter water floating on top of a lower, denser level. In spring and fall a phenomenon called "overturn" mixes the layers, redistributing nutrients, oxygen and plankton in the process.

Layering within lakes is the result of a curious property of water upon which all aquatic life depends. Like most other substances, water becomes more dense (and thus heavier) as it cools. But unlike most substances it becomes less dense when it cools below 39° Fahrenheit. As a result 39° water always sinks to the bottom of a lake while less dense water, which may be either cooler or warmer, floats above. If this did not happen lakes would freeze from the bottom to the top and life within them would be destroyed.

In winter, ice cover seals lake waters from the atmosphere and access to oxygen. Throughout this season oxygen within the lake is consumed by animals and decay organisms and relatively little excess is released by plants. Exhaustion of the oxygen supply in late winter and early spring may cause the death of fish and other aerobic organisms, a process known as winter kill. This situation is most prevalent in shallow, nutrient-rich lakes that enter the winter with little oxygen and use a great deal of their meager supply in the process of decay.

lake stratification and overturn

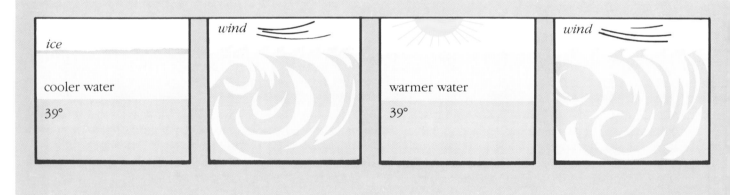

When spring arrives and the ice cover melts, upper waters are warmed to the same 39° temperature as the bottom and layering is broken. Winds then help mix all waters within the lake during spring overturn. Hot summer days continue to warm surface waters above 39° and the lake becomes layered again. The general cooling trend in fall leads to a homogeneous lake temperature and another overturn. Winter ice follows to complete the cycle.

Wherever sunlight penetrates to the bottom of a lake, rooted aquatic plants are able to grow. If the water is less than about six feet deep, plants often lift their flowers and leaves above the waves, otherwise they remain submerged. In deeper water, where the bottom falls off into darkness, plant and animal plankton float above in a bath of sunlight. Here plants use the energy of the sun to make food for themselves, releasing oxygen in the process. In this way the plants provide nourishment and oxygen that in turn supports all animal life.

Below this sunlit zone of watery pasture lands and clouds of single-celled grazers lies a deep, cool region where processes of decay recycle the nutrients that rain silently from above. Organic matter that settles into the ooze is broken down by fungi, bacteria, worms and other life forms that live within the land of the bottom-dwellers. Fish such as trout and bass swim freely within all the lake's zones, depending upon their particular temperature, oxygen and feeding requirements.

Not all Adirondack lakes and ponds trace their origins to the days of glaciation. In fact new ponds appear—and disappear—nearly every day. A few mountain lakes were formed by landslides that blocked streams flowing within the confines of a narrow, steep-sided defile. Others were left as oxbows by a restless river. Many large impoundments were created by men for recreation, hydropower and as millponds or reservoirs. Based on sheer numbers of projects, however, the prize dam builder in the region is nature's wonderful little engineer, the beaver.

Uncontrolled beaver trapping during the eighteenth and nineteenth centuries led to regional extirpation of the animal, but new populations were established by conservationists and continuing protection from overtrapping has allowed them to flourish once more. Since beavers returned at a time when Adirondack forests were recovering from the ravages of reckless logging and the wildfires that followed, the animals found conditions well-suited to their needs. Vast stands of sun-loving trees had grown up, providing an abundance of aspen bark, their favorite food. Young, tender, second-growth forests dominated the scene for many years and the beaver population exploded into its new-found Eden.

No other native animal has the power to purposefully manipulate its habitat the way beavers have. They gnaw through trees and shrubs and use them to dam sluggish streams and to raise the level of existing ponds and lakes. Surrounding lowlands are flooded, drowning the plants which grew there. Open water, marshes, swamps and wet meadows are formed. In this way beavers create a system of canals and waterways along which they float fresh-cut food sticks to the vicinity of their lodge. Some beavers dig homes within the banks of streams but most often they build a dome-shaped lodge of sticks and mud

A lingering wisp of morning mist burns away over Upper Ausable Lake, revealing the rock-slab windows of Gothics and the jagged ridge of Sawteeth.

©Gary Randorf 1977

within their pond. Here they live in relative safety, entering through an underwater passage that isolates them from marauding bears, coyotes and other predators.

Myriad forms of aquatic life, including plants, insects, crustaceans, mollusks, fish and microscopic free-floating plants and animals, move into the pond, adding to the diversity of the community. Storm waters are retained within the impoundment, reducing downstream flooding. Soil washed from uplands is detained on its journey to the sea. Numerous denizens of the surrounding forest come to the pond to drink and feed. For a time the beavers enjoy the bounty of their labors but as the years pass they find it increasingly difficult to get food. Eventually they move on in search of a new home with an ample supply of young woody growth.

During the next fifteen years or so the abandoned beaver pond recycles. The unrepaired dam deteriorates, then washes out and the pond drains away. Fresh sediments and organic debris form the seedbed for a lush growth of herbs, grasses, shrubs and trees. Sunshine pours onto this meadowland and plants pump moisture into the air, further drying the waterlogged soil. The old stream now meanders through a glade enriched by the efforts of those who have passed on. Just when it appears as though the forest will reclaim its lost ground forever a young pair of beavers wanders onto the scene and begins the process of change that is their birthright and our gain.

Sticks, mud, turf and even stones were used by beavers in the construction of this dam and lodge. In time, rising water will kill many surrounding trees, but most will be utilized for food and construction. The pond, called a flow, must be deep enough to prevent freezing to the bottom, for the beavers rely on an underwater cache of feed sticks to provide the bark which is their winter fare.

Propelled by its broad, horizontally flattened tail and webbed hind feet, a beaver cruises in home waters.

a.l.l.

Silhouettes of red spruce (left) and a pair of balsam firs frame this view from the eastern slope of Hurricane Mountain. Ascending branches and a conical shape distinguish balsams, while red spruce typically has more widely-spaced horizontal branches that turn up at the tip.

Slopes of Evergreen

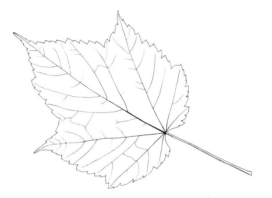

mountain maple

When you climb to altitudes above approximately 2,500 feet you pass into the boreal zone, where the plant and animal communities are similar to those found in the cold, moist, coniferous forests of Canada's Great North Woods. These are the climax forests of our high mountain slopes, the land of spruce and fir.

Development of a boreal forest in this region is largely controlled by soil, not temperature. Soils become increasingly shallow, infertile and wet at higher elevations and northern hardwoods lose vigor under these conditions. Beech, birch and maple are gradually replaced by red spruce and balsam fir. A forest composed primarily of yellow birch in the canopy and mountain maple in the understory marks the narrow transition zone or "ecotone" between the hardwood and spruce-fir communities, this change normally taking place within the 2,500 to 2,800 foot elevational band.

Relatively few species of plants have adapted to boreal life but those that have are quite abundant. Except for an occasional larch or northern white-cedar, red spruce and balsam fir are the only conifers you are likely to encounter on the upper spruce

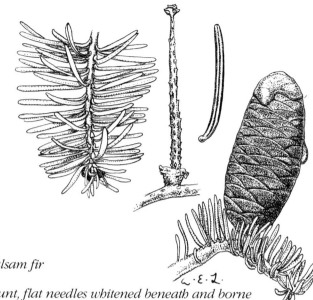

balsam fir

blunt, flat needles whitened beneath and borne on fleshy circular pads; scales fall from upright cones leaving a central wooden core

red spruce

sharp, square needles borne on woody pegs; pendant cones fall intact

slopes. Distinguishing these two trees is easy. Red spruce can be recognized by its sharp, dark yellow-green, four-sided needles and rough, brown bark. Where the needles have fallen from a twig tiny wooden pegs remain, forming a characteristic "sardine backbone." Balsam fir has blunt, shiny-green, flattened needles that are marked on the underside by two silvery lines. Small, round scars are left on bare twigs where each needle was attached. The bark of young trees is rather smooth and dull brownish-green, becoming blotched with gray as it ages. Numerous resin blisters cover the trunk and can be popped with a fingernail to release the sticky, aromatic fluid whose vapors fill the air with a fresh, heady scent.

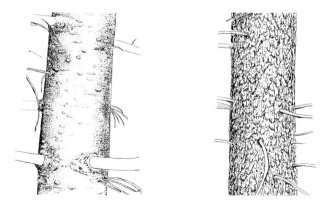

balsam fir   *details of bark*   *red spruce*

Bright red fruits of American mountain-ash add a splash of color to the boreal forest on Noonmark. From this perspective, it is easy to envision the local glacier that carved the amphitheater on Giant's western flank.

An even-aged stand of mountain paper birch towers over young spruces and firs along MacIntyre Brook. The birches seeded into mineral soil left by wildfire three-quarters of a century ago and they now foster the return of a boreal forest.

Paper (white) birch and mountain-ash are the major deciduous associates of spruce and fir. Both species are sun lovers that pioneer on burns and other disturbed sites throughout the Adirondacks. Paper birch, being more hardy and far more common, forms nearly pure stands over much of the heavily-burned High Peaks country. Mountain-ash tends to be most abundant along the upper limits of old burns, where it creates a linear pattern of small trees above solid patches of birch. It does not grow where a hot fire has burned deep into the humus, leaving only mineral soil—a situation in which birch thrives. Neither of these pioneers can hold a site for more than a generation, since they are intolerant of shade. During their tenure they act as a "nurse crop" for young spruces and firs by providing shade, humus and by generally moderating the harsh conditions that characterize sites of recent disturbance.

Partially-decayed needles, twigs and other debris accumulate beneath the deep shade of boreal conifers where decomposition is slowed by the cold, moist environment. A deep layer of organic duff covers the forest floor, overlying a thick band of dark, acidic, nutrient-poor humus and a shallow mineral soil. The ground is covered with a profusion of mosses and liverworts that thrive under these damp, shaded conditions by drawing nutrients and water directly into their leaves and bodies rather than through roots. Delicate plumes of mountain fern moss and scalelike ribbons of three-lobed Bazzania (a leafy liverwort) cover rocks, rotting logs and tree bases. Wood sorrel, the most common herb, can be recognized by its cloverlike foliage and brisk, acidic taste. Bunchberry, bluebead lily and spinulose woodfern account for most of the remaining species of conspicuous plants.

Sprigs of wood sorrel cover the ground beneath a bluebead lily and fronds of spinulose woodfern in this scene from the boreal forest.

Light from a blowdown penetrates the darkness that persists throughout the winter beneath the spruce and fir of a boreal community.

a boreal chickadee on old man's beard lichen

The harsh climate, infertile soil and lack of vegetational diversity on upper spruce slopes is reflected in the limited animal life of the boreal community. Many residents are northern specialties found nowhere else in New York State and some reach the southern limit of their entire breeding range within the park. Red squirrels are the mammal you are most likely to see, but numerous signs indicate the presence of varying (snowshoe) hares such as rounded scats and well-worn paths through the snow. Deer mice and masked shrews often search for food around campsites. Pine marten (American sable), once found throughout the state, are now restricted to the wildlands of the central Adirondacks, especially at higher elevations where they offer the opportunity for a rare sighting.

Boreal birdlife is similar to that found in coniferous swamps and bogs where spruce and fir are also dominant. Many of these birds have thin, high-pitched songs that can be distinguished by a characteristic rhythm or inflection. The blackpoll's song is a monotonous, thin lisp that is loudest toward the middle. Yellow-rumped warblers sing a wiry two-parted trill that either rises or falls at the end. Golden-crowned kinglets call "see-see-see" and sing a rising song that falls off into a weak chatter. For many people the loud, clear whistle of the white-throated sparrow symbolizes the North Country as he sings "old Sam Pea-body, Pea-body, Pea-body." Listen also for the breezy, flutelike songs of the thrushes. Swainson's thrush is more common at mid-elevations where it sings notes that tend to spiral upward, whereas the gray-cheeked thrush sings predominantly descending notes at dawn and dusk up near

A white-throated sparrow scratches for food in the snow.

Black spruce and balsam fir form an impenetrable elfin wood at the upper limit of the boreal forest. This is the treeline, an ecological tension zone beyond which trees can pass only as prostrate shrubs.

timberline. In clearings, blowdowns and other open areas look for the dark-eyed junco, which you can recognize by the bold flash of white on either side of its tail as the bird takes flight.

As the spruce slopes rise to the treeless summits above, a gradual but important change takes place. From about 4,000 feet upward, red spruce begins to drop out of the community, leaving a canopy composed almost entirely of balsam fir. The growing season is apparently too short for red spruce to grow quickly enough to compete with fir, maintain its vigor, set seed and reproduce itself. Near timberline all trees become stunted, windswept specimens that taper quickly from base to crown. Here, in an elfin wood, stems more than a century old may scarcely reach head-high. Black spruce at this elevation is sufficiently free of competition to join with fir for a short distance upward until they both crouch, kneel, then creep prostrate into the alpine zone beyond.

Lichen-encrusted boulders cast long shadows across golden clumps of deer's hair in an alpine meadow on Algonquin. ©Anne E. Lacy 1982

Islands in the Sky

At the end of the Ice Age the Adirondacks were colonized by communities of plants and animals similar to those now found in the arctic tundra far to the north. Ground-hugging shrubs, herbs, mosses and grass-like plants dominated the landscape. For a short time tundra-like vegetation held sway but as the climate moderated and soils developed, forests invaded the region. Nevertheless, small areas of arctic habitat are still found atop some of our highest mountain summits in what is called the alpine zone.

In all, about 85 acres of land on 11 major peaks are covered by alpine vegetation. Each site is an isolated outpost along the southernmost border of the community's range in the eastern United States. Most plants that try to establish a foothold here cannot stand the rigors of being alternately baked by the sun, moistened by fog and lashed by sand, ice and rain driven before a howling gale. Alpine species, survivors from the frigid Pleistocene Epoch, are therefore at an advantage since their unique adaptations help them in the struggle for existence under the severe conditions of their mountaintop environment.

The microclimate of alpine peaks is much more

Purple blooms of Lapland rosebay contrast with the white flowers of diapensia and the tiny catkins of bearberry willow in a bouquet of alpine wildflowers.

harsh than that found at the base of the mountains. For example, the mean annual temperature at the peak of Whiteface Mountain is about 10° colder than seven miles away in Lake Placid, which is 3,000 feet lower. This is exactly the difference in mean annual temperature between Lake Placid and Poughkeepsie, New York, about 200 miles farther south. The frost-free season on the summits is limited to approximately two months as compared to around 100 days in Lake Placid. Precipitation averages 25 percent more than in surrounding lowlands.

Nearly one-half of the total area above timberline consists of exposed rock, most of which is covered by lichens and mosses. These hardy pioneers are able to colonize bare mineral surfaces by gathering nutrients from rain, dust and decayed fragments of their own tissues. Lichens also secrete acids that help dissolve substances from the rocks on which they live. Each different organism is adapted to a slightly different set of environmental conditions. Rock mosses live in the moist micro-valleys while lichens cover the drier, more exposed micro-ridges on bedrock and boulders. Life for these organisms is so demanding that they grow very slowly but may live an astonishingly long time. Some individual alpine lichens are perhaps several thousand years old.

Alpine pioneers modify their environment in many ways. They provide a source of nutrients, shade from sun, protection from wind and a supply of moisture that enables other plants to grow in their place. Gradually a carpet of different mosses, lichens and herbs spreads over the rock. Sphagnum moss soon infiltrates this carpet and becomes dominant. The thirsty sphagnum adds a great deal of living and dead material to the community which then acts like a blotter in the sky, drinking moisture from rain, dew and clouds. Soil composed largely of organic duff thickens, acidifies and forms the matrix in which woody-stemmed heath plants and dwarf trees become established. In many ways alpine summits are like inverted bogs, covering a lofty dome rather than a lowland depression.

Wind is perhaps the most important factor in determining which plants will eventually live on a particular site. Sharply-angled rocks that jut above their surroundings into the full blast of the wind may pass thousands of years with little more than a scant covering of lichens and tiny mosses. Close to the surface of the ground, wind, temperature and moisture extremes are less severe. In these areas compact colonies of shrubby "cushion plants" such as

Transformed into a living tapestry by the frosts of late summer, the alpine community of Algonquin Peak rises above the krummholz. Fingers of boreal vegetation reach toward the summit on southeastern exposures, but the pattern is reversed on the opposite side due to the drying effect of prevailing winds.

Wind smashing into this rock ledge dries leafy plants as effectively as a blowtorch, leaving only lichens and tiny rock mosses to grow in the relatively still air near the surface. Gold-colored deer's hair shields the purplish alpine bilberry which is more easily desiccated.

Lapland rosebay and Diapensia add a delicate splash of color to alpine gardens. On bare soil and in pockets of muck and gravelly sand, clumps of mountain sandwort seem to defy the elements with their long-lasting white blooms. Relatively level, exposed sites are likely to accumulate enough soil and moisture to foster development of a grassy meadow composed of Bigelow sedge, deer's hair and the sweet-smelling alpine holygrass.

Depressions in the bedrock and sites in the lee of ridges and boulders usually have a dependable snowpack and it is here that sphagnum helps create a true heath community. Winter protection under a blanket of snow is essential for the growth of shrubs that have perennial stems more than a few inches high. If this covering is blown away buds and twigs are dried beyond recovery at a time when the frozen ground prevents replacement of precious moisture.

A dark-eyed junco searches for seeds near a dwarf bearberry willow above timberline.

Mountain sandwort (left) and three-toothed cinquefoil bloom in the austerity of gravelly sand.

Alpine bilberry, the most abundant plant above timberline, is pictured above twin stems of Labrador tea and a clump of black crowberry. Of the three shrubs, only Labrador tea can be found in lowland bogs.

Alpine bilberry, a relative of lowland blueberries, prefers this habitat which it shares with such familiar bog-dwellers as leatherleaf, Labrador tea and bog laurel. Many alpine specialties are found here too, including black crowberry, a diminutive variety of cotton grass called hare's-tail, dwarf birch, and bearberry willow that has fuzzy catkins like its lowland pussy willow cousins but only grows a few inches high.

Plants from the boreal community are able to penetrate the alpine zone within deep bedrock fissures and under the shelter of ledges and boulders. Balsam fir, mountain paper birch and mountain alder are common. Bunchberry, bluebead lily, twinflower, bristly clubmoss, false hellebore and a variety of mosses crowd beneath the shrubby overstory. Far from its lowland haunts, black spruce is at home here, where conditions are suitable to its sun-loving, acid-tolerant, low-nutrient lifestyle. Since these plants are unable to thrive when exposed to winter winds, their branches seldom extend much beyond the confines of protected microhabitats. Wherever terminal shoots of trees poke above the snow they are dried to death. Ground-hugging lateral branches survive, however, and mats of foliage extend from gnarled, twisted, bonsai-like trunks, a form called

Dark rock mosses fill the micro-valleys, while yellow lichens cover the drier ridges on a steep bedrock exposure in the alpine zone. Deer's hair is growing within green pincushions of diapensia and sprawling branches of alpine bilberry in a small pocket of soil, above.

Krummholz forms under the most severe conditions upright trees can withstand. Here in the alpine zone they become gnarled veterans of continuing battles with the elements until, in death, their bleached skeletons protect a new generation of replacements.

"krummholz," from the German words meaning crooked wood.

Even though alpine plants have adapted to harsh microclimatic conditions they live within a fragile community that is easily damaged by natural or man-made forces. Wildfires have eliminated many species. Air pollution now threatens delicate lichens. Hiking boots cause great harm to the shallow, peaty turf and once this mat is cut, water erodes it quickly. Organic matter that has taken perhaps thousands of years to accumulate is then washed away, leaving a naked scar that widens at a frightening rate. But this situation is changing. Work is underway to stabilize damaged areas by fertilizing, planting grasses and by confining visitors to marked pathways.

The only birds you are likely to see near the ground on barren mountaintops are dark-eyed juncos and perhaps a white-throated sparrow or two. Neither bird breeds above timberline but they feed here on seeds, berries and scraps of food left by visitors.

White-throats whistle a loud, clear song, whereas the juncos limit their vocalizing to a soft, bell-like tinkling trill or a metallic "tink-tink-tink." The white outer tail feathers of the junco can be seen at a distance but you must be closer to see the sparrow's white throat.

Common ravens are returning to the Adirondacks from which they were nearly extirpated early in the century and you may be fortunate enough to spot one. Like crows, these black scavengers of the high country usually travel in family groups but are much larger than their lowland cousins. Size may be difficult to judge at a distance so listen carefully for the gutteral croaks and loud squawks that distinguish the raven's calls from the familiar "caw" of the crow. If you have binoculars look closely at the tail. It is fan-shaped on crows but narrows slightly at both ends on ravens to give a wedged appearance. Ravens are superb acrobats and seldom fly for long without twisting and tumbling in aerial maneuvers over these fog-shrouded islands in the sky.

At close range, the strong bill and shaggy neck feathers of a common raven are apparent.

We have our little air holes in the cities, which we call parks, and we have some sections of the west roped off by law which the east is welcome to roam over if it can pay the carfare to them. But it has remained for New York State to set aside more than a tithe of its total area where men and women can seek sanctuary from cities and heat and the everlasting press of things. And New York State has done more. She has not only offered her mountains and lakes and woods to the tired student from Ithaca, the tired philosopher from the Hub, the tired businessman from everywhere, but she has made trails through the mountains, has stocked the streams and lakes, and is doing her best to preserve the forest. The citizens of the State pay for this, and anybody can enjoy their gift for a thank-you. All that they request is care in the enjoyment. Great care is the least return that we can make.

T. MORRIS LONGSTRETH, 1917
THE ADIRONDACKS

Canoeist on Pharaoh Lake

©Gary Randorf 1980

white fringed orchid

Acknowledgments

The author and illustrator are deeply indebted to our friends and professional colleagues who gave freely of their time and expertise in the preparation of the Wildguide. In particular, we wish to thank Timothy L. Barnett, Executive Director of the Adirondack Conservancy and Gary Randorf, Executive Director of The Adirondack Council for their unfailing support of our project and ceaseless efforts on our behalf. Without their help the Wildguide would not have been initiated, researched or completed.

We owe a sincere debt of gratitude to the members and Boards of Directors of The Adirondack Council, Frances Beinecke, Chairwoman, and the Adirondack Conservancy, Wayne H. Byrne, Chairman, for their generous contributions of funding and staff support.

Numerous persons assisted us in field work and in the gathering and interpretation of scientific information, especially Greenleaf Chase of Saranac Lake and Michael Kudish, Paul Smith's College, both of whom also reviewed the entire manuscript. Others who made valuable technical contributions include Drs. Paul F. Connor, Robert J. Dineen, Yngvar W. Isachsen, Timothy L. McCabe, Richard Mitchell, Richard H. Monheimer and cartographer John B. Skiba, all of the State Science Service, New York State Museum; Drs. Paul J. Spangler and Richard Zusi of the Smithsonian Institution; William Crowley and Tracy N. Meehan of the Adirondack Museum; Dr. Richard Andrus, SUNY Binghamton; Michael Boss; Dr. Thomas C. Field, Fernwood—Limne, Inc.; Dr. Edwin H. Ketchledge, SUNY College of Environmental Science and Forestry; Dr. Gordon L. Kirkland, Shippensburg College; A. Lang Elliott; Bruce Milne; Richard A. Rowlett; and Dr. Ian Worley, University of Vermont.

The illustration on page 65 is based on a photograph by Dorothy Crumb and those on pages 70 and 108 on photographs by B. D. Cottrille. Permission for their use is through the courtesy of the Cornell Laboratory of Ornithology. The cover illustration was based in part on photographs courtesy of The North American Loon Fund.

Artistic advice was received from Charles Anthony, Sue E. Dodge, Maria C. Halton, M. Kyle McLellan, Beki Maurello, Patricia A. Taber, Robert J. Wagner, Michelle Wilcox, and especially from Kathryn M. Conway.

The book was edited by Joseph Kastner and proofread by Helen Deuell. Additional editorial contributions were made by Richard Beamish and Robert F. Hall. Carolyn Conklin and Helen Paul each typed numerous versions of the manuscript.

Accommodations for living and work space during our years in the Adirondacks were graciously provided by the Board of the Bruce L. Crary Foundation, Richard W. Lawrence, Jr., Chairman. We shall always treasure the memories of our days at the Hand House and the friendships we made there.

Appendix

Checklist of Fishes

compiled by Jerry Platt

The following list is compiled primarily on the basis of specimens and records at the New York State Museum, or from credible reports in the literature.

Nomenclature follows that given in *A List of Common and Scientific Names of Fishes from the United States and Canada,* by C. R. Robins, R. M. Bailey, C. E. Bond, J. R. Brooker, E. A. Lachner, R. N. Lea and W. B. Scott, American Fisheries Society, Special Publication No. 12, 1980.

blacknose dace

*Species restricted in distribution to Lake Champlain or to the Lake and the lower reaches of its larger streams.

Petromyzontidae   Lampreys
Ichthyomyzon unicuspis   silver lamprey
Lampetra appendix   American brook lamprey
Petromyzon marinus   sea lamprey

Acipenseridae   Sturgeons
Acipenser fulvescens   lake sturgeon

Lepisosteidae   Gars
Lepisosteus osseus   longnose gar

Amiidae   Bowfins
Amia calva   bowfin

Anguillidae   Freshwater Eels
Anguilla rostrata   American eel

Clupeidae   Herrings
Alosa aestivalis   blueback herring
Alosa pseudoharengus   alewife

Hiodontidae   Mooneyes
Hiodon tergisus   mooneye

Salmonidae   Trouts
Coregonus artedii   cisco or lake herring
Coregonus clupeaformis   lake whitefish
Oncorhynchus nerka   kokanee
Prosopium cylindraceum   round whitefish
Salmo gairdneri   rainbow trout
Salmo salar   Atlantic salmon
Salmo trutta   brown trout
Salvelinus fontinalis   brook trout
Salvelinus namaycush   lake trout

Osmeridae   Smelts
Osmerus mordax   rainbow smelt

Umbridae   Mudminnow
Umbra limi   central mudminnow

Esocidae   Pikes
Esox americanus americanus   redfin pickerel
Esox lucius   northern pike
Esox masquinongy   muskellunge
Esox niger   chain pickerel

Cyprinidae   Carps and Minnows
Carassius auratus   goldfish
Couesius plumbeus   lake chub
Cyprinus carpio   common carp
Exoglossum maxillingua   cutlips minnow
Hybognathus regius   eastern silvery minnow
Hybognathus hankinsoni   brassy minnow
Notemigonus crysoleucas   golden shiner
Notropis atherinoides   emerald shiner
Notropis bifrenatus   bridle shiner
Notropis cornutus   common shiner
Notropis heterodon   blackchin shiner
Notropis heterolepis   blacknose shiner
Notropis hudsonius   spottail shiner
Notropis rubellus   rosyface shiner
Notropis spilopterus   spotfin shiner
Notropis stramineus   sand shiner
Notropis volucellus   mimic shiner
Phoxinus eos   northern redbelly dace
Phoxinus neogaeus   finescale dace
Pimephales notatus   bluntnose minnow
Pimephales promelas   fathead minnow

Rhinichthys atratulus   blacknose dace
Rhinichthys cataractae   longnose dace
Semotilus atromaculatus   creek chub
Semotilus corporalis   fallfish
Semotilus margarita   pearl dace

Catostomidae   Suckers
 Catostomus catostomus   longnose sucker
 Catostomus commersoni   white sucker
*Moxostoma anisurum   silver redhorse
*Moxostoma macrolepidotum   shorthead redhorse

Ictaluridae   Bullhead catfishes
 Ictalurus natalis   yellow bullhead
 Ictalurus nebulosus   brown bullhead
*Ictalurus punctatus   channel catfish
 Noturus flavus   stonecat
 Noturus gyrinus   tadpole madtom
 Noturus insignis   margined madtom

Percopsidae   Trout-Perches
*Percopsis omiscomaycus   trout-perch

Gadidae   Codfishes
*Lota lota   burbot

Cyprinodontidae   Killifishes
 Fundulus diaphanus   banded killifish

Gasterosteidae   Sticklebacks
 Culaea inconstans   brook stickleback

Centrarchidae   Sunfishes
 Ambloplites rupestris   rock bass
 Lepomis auritus   redbreast sunfish
 Lepomis gibbosus   pumpkinseed
 Lepomis macrochirus   bluegill
 Micropterus dolomieui   smallmouth bass
 Micropterus salmoides   largemouth bass
 Pomoxis nigromaculatus   black crappie

Percidae   Perches
 Etheostoma flabellare   fantail darter
 Etheostoma olmstedi   tessellated darter
*Percina caprodes   logperch
*Percina copelandi   channel darter
 Perca flavescens   yellow perch
*Stizostedion canadense   sauger
 Stizostedion vitreum vitreum   walleye

Sciaenidae   Drums
*Aplodinotus grunniens   freshwater drum

Cottidae   Sculpins
*Cottus bairdi   mottled sculpin
 Cottus cognatus   slimy sculpin

Checklists of Amphibians and Reptiles

compiled by Jerry Platt

The following lists are compiled primarily on the basis of specimens and records at the New York State Museum.

Scientific and common names of amphibians and reptiles are as given in *Standard Common and Current Scientific Names for North American Amphibians and Reptiles,* by J. T. Collins, J. E. Huheey, J. L. Knight and H. M. Smith, Society for the Study of Amphibians and Reptiles, Misc. Pub., Herpetological Circular No. 7, 1978.

*Species believed to be extirpated from the park.

AMPHIBIANS

Ambystoma jeffersonianum   Jefferson salamander
Ambystoma maculatum   spotted salamander
Desmognathus fuscus   dusky salamander
Desmognathus ochrophaeus   mountain dusky salamander
Eurycea bislineata   two-lined salamander
Gyrinophilus porphyriticus   spring salamander
Hemidactylium scutatum   four-toed salamander
Necturus maculosus   mudpuppy
Notophthalmus viridescens   eastern newt
Plethodon cinereus   redback salamander
Bufo americanus   American toad

AMPHIBIANS, continued ...

Hyla crucifer   spring peeper
Hyla versicolor   gray treefrog
Rana catesbeiana   bullfrog
Rana clamitans   green frog
Rana palustris   pickerel frog
Rana pipiens   northern leopard frog
Rana septentrionalis   mink frog
Rana sylvatica   wood frog

REPTILES

Chelydra serpentina   snapping turtle
Chrysemys picta   painted turtle
Clemmys guttata   spotted turtle
Clemmys insculpta   wood turtle
Clemmys muhlenbergi   bog turtle
Graptemys geographica   map turtle
Eumeces fasciatus   five-lined skink
Crotalus horridus   timber rattlesnake
Diadophis punctatus   ringneck snake
Lampropeltis triangulum   milk snake
Nerodia sipedon   northern water snake
Opheodrys vernalis   smooth green snake
Storeria dekayi   brown snake
Storeria occipitomaculata   redbelly snake
Thamnophis sauritus   eastern ribbon snake
Thamnophis sirtalis   common garter snake

Checklist of Birds

compiled by John M. C. Peterson

This list provides a compilation of all species of birds recorded in the Adirondack Park through 1983, using the sequence, taxonomy, and English names of the American Ornithologists' Union *Check-List of North American Birds* (6th ed., 1983). All species have been accepted and published elsewhere with appropriate documentation, and each has been reviewed by the compiler for accuracy. Only full species are included; recognizable subspecies (such as "Northern" and "Prairie" Horned Larks, "Western" and "Yellow" Palm Warblers), hybrids (American Black Duck x Mallard, "Lawrence's Warbler"), and morphs ("Blue Goose") are omitted. Also omitted are species reported from the Adirondack Park with insufficient documentation and presumed escaped exotic species. Examples of the latter include Ringed Turtle-Dove (recognized by the A.O.U.) and Blossom-headed Parakeet (not listed by the A.O.U.).

Visitant species are those which nest only outside the Adirondack Park. All others might be considered breeding species, although several no longer nest in the Adirondack region, and others do so only occasionally or within an extremely restricted range inside the Blue Line boundaries. Status is based upon historic evidence; recent field work, including that in progress for an Atlas of breeding birds of New York State; and, where more solid evidence is still lacking, personal judgment. Any errors of omission or inclusion are those of the compiler. Some 297 species are listed, of which 193 are presumed to breed, or have bred. One, the Northern Bobwhite, is apparently extirpated; the last specimen was secured at Willsboro, Essex County, in 1893. Another, the Passenger Pigeon, is now extinct, with the last Adirondack specimen collected at Willsboro in 1891.

Noteworthy sightings of Adirondack Park birds may be reported to High Peaks Audubon Society, Inc., Elizabethtown, NY 12932.

†   Visitant Species only
*   Introduced Species
‡   Extinct Species

White-throated sparrow

†Red-throated Loon
Common Loon
Pied-billed Grebe
†Horned Grebe
†Red-necked Grebe
†Eared Grebe
†Western Grebe
†Leach's Storm-Petrel
†American White Pelican
†Double-crested Cormorant
American Bittern
Least Bittern
Great Blue Heron
†Great Egret
†Snowy Egret
†Tricolored Heron
Cattle Egret
Green-backed Heron
Black-crowned Night-
  Heron
†Tundra Swan
*Mute Swan
†Snow Goose
†Brant
Canada Goose
Wood Duck
Green-winged Teal
American Black Duck
Mallard
Northern Pintail
Blue-winged Teal
†Northern Shoveler
Gadwall
†American Wigeon

†Canvasback
Redhead
Ring-necked Duck
†Greater Scaup
†Lesser Scaup
†King Eider
†Harlequin Duck
†Oldsquaw
†Black Scoter
†Surf Scoter
†White-winged Scoter
Common Goldeneye
†Barrow's Goldeneye
†Bufflehead
Hooded Merganser
Common Merganser
Red-breasted Merganser
†Ruddy Duck
Turkey Vulture
Osprey
Bald Eagle
Northern Harrier
Sharp-shinned Hawk
Cooper's Hawk
Northern Goshawk
Red-shouldered Hawk
Broad-winged Hawk
Red-tailed Hawk
†Rough-legged Hawk
Golden Eagle
American Kestrel
†Merlin
Peregrine Falcon
†Gyrfalcon

*Gray Partridge
*Ring-necked Pheasant
Spruce Grouse
Ruffed Grouse
Wild Turkey
Northern Bobwhite
†King Rail
Virginia Rail
Sora
Common Moorhen
American Coot
†Black-bellied Plover
†Lesser Golden-Plover
†Semipalmated Plover
Killdeer
†Greater Yellowlegs
†Lesser Yellowlegs
†Solitary Sandpiper
†Willet
Spotted Sandpiper
Upland Sandpiper
†Whimbrel
†Ruddy Turnstone
†Red Knot
†Sanderling
†Semipalmated Sandpiper
†Western Sandpiper
†Least Sandpiper
†White-rumped Sandpiper
†Baird's Sandpiper
†Pectoral Sandpiper
†Purple Sandpiper
†Dunlin
†Buff-breasted Sandpiper

†Short-billed Dowitcher
†Long-billed
  Dowitcher
 Common Snipe
 American Woodcock
†Wilson's Phalarope
†Red-necked Phalarope
†Red Phalarope
†Pomarine Jaeger
†Parasitic Jaeger
†Long-tailed Jaeger
†Little Gull
†Bonaparte's Gull
 Ring-billed Gull
 Herring Gull
†Iceland Gull
†Lesser Black-backed Gull
†Glaucous Gull
 Great Black-backed Gull
†Sabine's Gull
†Caspian Tern
†Common Tern
†Sooty Tern
 Black Tern
†Dovekie
†Thick-billed Murre
†Black Guillemot
*Rock Dove
 Mourning Dove
‡Passenger Pigeon
 Black-billed Cuckoo
 Yellow-billed Cuckoo
 Common Barn-Owl
 Eastern Screech-Owl

 Great Horned Owl
†Snowy Owl
†Northern Hawk-Owl
 Barred Owl
†Great Gray Owl
 Long-eared Owl
 Short-eared Owl
†Boreal Owl
 Northern Saw-whet Owl
 Common Nighthawk
 Whip-poor-will
 Chimney Swift
 Ruby-throated Hummingbird
†Rufous Hummingbird
 Belted Kingfisher
 Red-headed Woodpecker
 Yellow-bellied Sapsucker
 Downy Woodpecker
 Hairy Woodpecker
 Three-toed Woodpecker
 Black-backed Woodpecker
 Northern Flicker
 Pileated Woodpecker
 Olive-sided Flycatcher
 Eastern Wood-Pewee
 Yellow-bellied Flycatcher
 Alder Flycatcher
 Willow Flycatcher
 Least Flycatcher
 Eastern Phoebe
 Great Crested Flycatcher
 Eastern Kingbird
 Horned Lark
 Purple Martin

 Tree Swallow
 Northern Rough-winged Swallow
 Bank Swallow
 Cliff Swallow
 Barn Swallow
 Gray Jay
 Blue Jay
 American Crow
 Common Raven
 Black-capped Chickadee
 Boreal Chickadee
 Tufted Titmouse
 Red-breasted Nuthatch
 White-breasted Nuthatch
 Brown Creeper
 Carolina Wren
 House Wren
 Winter Wren
 Sedge Wren
 Marsh Wren
 Golden-crowned Kinglet
 Ruby-crowned Kinglet
 Blue-gray Gnatcatcher
†Northern Wheatear
 Eastern Bluebird
 Veery
 Gray-cheeked Thrush
 Swainson's Thrush
 Hermit Thrush
 Wood Thrush
 American Robin
 Gray Catbird
 Northern Mockingbird
 Brown Thrasher

†Water Pipit
†Bohemian Waxwing
Cedar Waxwing
†Northern Shrike
Loggerhead Shrike
*European Starling
White-eyed Vireo
Solitary Vireo
Yellow-throated Vireo
Warbling Vireo
Philadelphia Vireo
Red-eyed Vireo
†Blue-winged Warbler
Golden-winged Warbler
Tennessee Warbler
†Orange-crowned Warbler
Nashville Warbler
Northern Parula
Yellow Warbler
Chestnut-sided Warbler
Magnolia Warbler
Cape May Warbler
Black-throated Blue Warbler
Yellow-rumped Warbler
Black-throated Green Warbler
Blackburnian Warbler
†Yellow-throated Warbler
Pine Warbler
Prairie Warbler
Palm Warbler
Bay-breasted Warbler
Blackpoll Warbler
Cerulean Warbler
Black-and-white Warbler

American Redstart
†Prothonotary Warbler
†Worm-eating Warbler
Ovenbird
Northern Waterthrush
Louisiana Waterthrush
†Kentucky Warbler
†Connecticut Warbler
Mourning Warbler
Common Yellowthroat
Wilson's Warbler
Canada Warbler
Yellow-breasted Chat
†Summer Tanager
Scarlet Tanager
Northern Cardinal
Rose-breasted Grosbeak
†Blue Grosbeak
Indigo Bunting
†Dickcissel
Rufous-sided Towhee
†American Tree Sparrow
Chipping Sparrow
Clay-colored Sparrow
Field Sparrow
Vesper Sparrow
†Lark Sparrow
Savannah Sparrow
Grasshopper Sparrow
†Sharp-tailed
  Sparrow
†Fox Sparrow
Song Sparrow
Lincoln's Sparrow

Swamp Sparrow
White-throated Sparrow
†White-crowned Sparrow
†Harris' Sparrow
Dark-eyed Junco
†Lapland Longspur
†Snow Bunting
Bobolink
Red-winged Blackbird
Eastern Meadowlark
†Yellow-headed Blackbird
Rusty Blackbird
Common Grackle
Brown-headed Cowbird
Orchard Oriole
Northern Oriole
†Brambling
†Pine Grosbeak
Purple Finch
House Finch
Red Crossbill
White-winged Crossbill
†Common Redpoll
†Hoary Redpoll
Pine Siskin
American Goldfinch
Evening Grosbeak
*House Sparrow

†   Visitant Species only
*   Introduced Species
‡   Extinct Species

Checklist of Mammals

compiled by Jerry Platt

The following list is compiled primarily on the basis of museum specimens and records or from credible reports in the literature. Information was gained from a search of the Zoology files at the New York State Museum, augmented by records from Cornell University, the Museum of Comparative Zoology, the National Museum of Natural History, Shippensburg College, and the University of Michigan.

Nomenclature for mammals follows that given in *Revised Checklist of North American Mammals North of Mexico,* by J. K. Jones, D. C. Carter, and H. H. Genoways, Texas Tech. University, 1979.

muskrat push-up

*Species believed to be extirpated from the park.

Didelphis virginiana   Virginia oppossum
Sorex cinereus   masked shrew
Sorex palustris   water shrew
Sorex fumeus   smoky shrew
Sorex dispar   long-tailed shrew
Microsorex hoyi   pygmy shrew
Blarina brevicauda   short-tailed shrew
Parascalops breweri   hairy-tailed mole
Condylura cristata   star-nosed mole
Myotis lucifugus   little brown myotis
Myotis keenii   Keen's myotis
Myotis sodalis   Indiana bat
Myotis leibii   small-footed myotis
Lasionycteris noctivagans   silver-haired bat
Pipistrellus subflavus   eastern pipistrelle
Eptesicus fuscus   big brown bat
Lasiurus cinereus   hoary bat
Sylvilagus floridanus   eastern cottontail
Sylvilagus transitionalis   New England cottontail
Lepus americanus   snowshoe hare
Tamias striatus   eastern chipmunk
Marmota monax   woodchuck
Sciurus carolinensis   gray squirrel
Tamiasciurus hudsonicus   red squirrel
Glaucomys volans   southern flying squirrel
Glaucomys sabrinus   northern flying squirrel
Castor canadensis   beaver
Peromyscus maniculatus   deer mouse
Peromyscus leucopus   white-footed mouse
Clethrionomys gapperi   southern red-backed vole
Microtus pennsylvanicus   meadow vole
Microtus chrotorrhinus   rock vole
Microtus pinetorum   woodland vole
Ondatra zibethicus   muskrat

Synaptomys cooperi   southern bog lemming
Rattus norvegicus   Norway rat
Mus musculus   house mouse
Zapus hudsonius   meadow jumping mouse
Napaeozapus insignis   woodland jumping mouse
Erethizon dorsatum   porcupine
Canis latrans   coyote
Canis lupus   gray wolf
Vulpes vulpes   red fox
Urocyon cinereoargenteus   gray fox
Ursus americanus   black bear
Procyon lotor   raccoon
Martes americana   marten
Martes pennanti   fisher
Mustela erminea   ermine
Mustela frenata   long-tailed weasel
Mustela vison   mink
Mephitis mephitis   striped skunk
Lutra canadensis   river otter
Felis concolor   mountain lion
Felis lynx   lynx
Felis rufus   bobcat
Cervus elaphus   wapiti or elk
Odocoileus virginianus   white-tailed deer
Alces alces   moose

139

Checklist of Trees

compiled by Michael G. DiNunzio
and Beth Yanuck-Platt

Trees are defined here as woody plants reaching a minimum height of twelve feet and a minimum diameter (at 4-1/2 feet above ground level) of three inches wherever they may occur naturally. Records at the Office of the State Botanist, New York State Museum and Science Service, Albany, were used to confirm the presence of all checklist species within the Adirondack Park.

Scientific names are as given in *A Synonymized Checklist of the Vascular Flora of the United States, Canada, and Greenland,* by John T. and R. Kartesz, University of North Carolina Press, Chapel Hill, 1980. Common names are as given in *Checklist of Native and Naturalized Trees of the United States (Including Alaska),* Agricultural Handbook No. 41, E. L. Little, Jr., 1953.

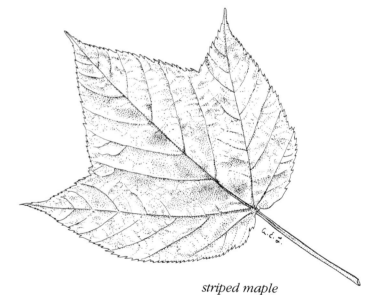

striped maple

Common naturalized or plantation species are indicated by an asterisk (*).

CUPRESSACEAE   Cedar or Cypress Family
Juniperus virginiana   eastern redcedar
Thuja occidentalis   northern white-cedar

PINACEAE   Pine Family
Abies balsamea   balsam fir
Larix laricina   tamarack (eastern larch)
*Picea abies   Norway spruce
Picea glauca   white spruce
Picea mariana   black spruce
Picea rubens   red spruce
Pinus banksiana   jack pine
Pinus resinosa   red pine
Pinus rigida   pitch pine
Pinus strobus   eastern white pine
*Pinus sylvestris   Scots (Scotch) pine
Tsuga canadensis   eastern hemlock

SALICACEAE   Willow Family
*Populus alba   white poplar
Populus balsamifera   balsam poplar
Populus deltoides   eastern cottonwood
Populus grandidentata   bigtooth aspen
*Populus nigra var. italica   Lombardy poplar
Populus tremuloides   quaking aspen
*Salix alba   white willow
Salix amygdaloides   peachleaf willow
*Salix babylonica   weeping willow
Salix bebbiana   Bebb willow
Salix discolor   pussy willow

*Salix fragilis   crack willow
Salix lucida   shining willow
Salix nigra   black willow

JUGLANDACEAE   Walnut Family
Carya cordiformis   bitternut hickory
Carya ovalis   red hickory
Carya ovata   shagbark hickory
Juglans cinerea   butternut
*Juglans nigra   black walnut

BETULACEAE   Birch Family
Alnus incana   speckled alder
Betula alleghaniensis   yellow birch
Betula cordifolia   mountain paper birch
Betula lenta   sweet birch
Betula papyrifera   paper birch
Betula populifolia   gray birch
Carpinus caroliniana   American hornbeam
Ostrya virginiana   eastern hophornbeam

FAGACEAE   Beech Family
Castanea dentata   American chestnut
Fagus grandifolia   American beech
Quercus alba   white oak
Quercus bicolor   swamp white oak
Quercus macrocarpa   bur oak
Quercus montana   chestnut oak
Quercus rubra   northern red oak
Quercus velutina   black oak

ULMACEAE   Elm Family
 Celtis occidentalis   hackberry
 Ulmus americana   American elm
 Ulmus rubra   slippery elm
 Ulmus thomasii   rock elm

LAURACEAE   Laurel Family
 Sassafras albidum   sassafras

HAMAMELIDACEAE   Witch-hazel Family
 Hamamelis virginiana   witch-hazel
 *Liquidambar styraciflua   sweetgum

PLATANACEAE   Plane-tree Family
 Platanus occidentalis   American sycamore

ROSACEAE   Rose Family
 Amelanchier arborea   downy serviceberry
 Crataegus spp.   hawthorn (many species of great
   taxonomic complexity)
 Malus pumila   apple
 Prunus pensylvanica   pin (fire) cherry
 Prunus serotina   black cherry
 Prunus virginiana   common chokecherry
 *Pyrus communis   pear
 Sorbus americana   American mountain-ash
 Sorbus decora   showy mountain-ash

FABACEAE   Legume or Pea Family
 *Robinia pseudoacacia   black locust

ANACARDIACEAE   Cashew Family
 Rhus glabra   smooth sumac
 Rhus typhina   staghorn sumac

ACERACEAE   Maple Family
 *Acer negundo   boxelder
 Acer nigrum   black maple
 Acer pensylvanicum   striped maple
 Acer rubrum   red maple
 Acer saccharinum   silver maple
 Acer saccharum   sugar maple
 Acer spicatum   mountain maple

RHAMNACEAE   Buckthorn Family
 *Rhamnus cathartica   European buckthorn

TILIACEAE   Linden Family
 Tilia americana   American basswood

NYSSACEAE   Sour Gum Family
 Nyssa sylvatica   black tupelo

OLEACEAE   Olive Family
 Fraxinus americana   white ash
 Fraxinus nigra   black ash
 Fraxinus pennsylvanica   green (red) ash

For Reading and Reference

Adirondack Park Agency and New York State Department of Environmental Conservation. *A Natural History of the Adirondack Park, NY,* 1979

Barnett, Lincoln. *The Ancient Adirondacks.* Time-Life Books, New York, 1974

Beehler, Bruce McP. *Birdlife of the Adirondack Park.* Adirondack Mountain Club, Glens Falls, NY, 1978

Borror, Donald J. and R. E. White. *A Field Guide to the Insects of America North of Mexico.* Houghton Mifflin Company, Boston, 1970

Brockman, C. Frank. *Trees of North America: A Field Guide to the Major Native and Introduced Species North of Mexico.* Golden Press, New York, 1968

Broughton, J. G. and others. *Geology of New York State: A Short Account.* New York State Museum and Science Service. Educational Leaflet 20. 49 pp. and colored map, 1966

Burt, William H. and R. P. Grossenheider. *A Field Guide to the Mammals.* Houghton Mifflin Company, Boston, 1964

Carleton, Geoffrey. *Birds of Essex County, New York.* High Peaks Audubon Society, Elizabethtown, NY, 1980

Cobb, Boughton. *A Field Guide to the Ferns and Their Related Families of Northeastern and Central North America.* Houghton Mifflin Company, Boston, 1963

Conant, Roger. *A Field Guide to Reptiles and Amphibians of the United States and Canada East of the 100th Meridian.* Houghton Mifflin Company, Boston, 1958

Davis, George D. *Man and the Adirondack Environment: A Primer.* Adirondack Museum, Blue Mountain Lake, New York, 1977

Fisher, Donald W., Y. W. Isachsen, and P. R. Whitney. *New Mountains from Old Rocks: The Adirondacks.* New York State Museum and Science Service. Educational Leaflet 23, 1980 (revised)

George, Carl J. *The Fishes of the Adirondack Park.* New York State Department of Environmental Conservation, Albany, 1980

Isachsen, Y. W. *Continental Collisions and Ancient Volcanoes: The Geology of Southeastern New York.* New York State Museum and Science Service. Educational Leaflet 24, 1980

Ketchledge, E. H. "Trees and Forests of the Adirondacks," in *The Adirondack High Peaks and the Forty-Sixers.* Pp. 199–213. The Peters Print, Albany, 1970

Ketchledge, E. H. *Trees of the Adirondack High Peak Region: A Hiker's Guide.* Adirondack Mountain Club, Glens Falls, New York, 1967.

Klein, Harold G. "Mammals of the High Peak Area," in *The Adirondack High Peaks and the Forty-Sixers.* Pp. 217–266. The Peters Print, Albany, 1970

Kudish, Michael. *Paul Smith's Flora. Vol. I: A Preliminary Vascular Flora of the Paul Smiths–Saranac Lake Area, the Adirondacks, New York, with Notes on the Climate, Geology, and Soils. Vol. II: Additional Vascular Plants, Bryophytes (Mosses and Liverworts), Soils and Vegetation, Local History.* Paul Smith's College, Paul Smiths, New York, 1975 (Vol. I), 1981 (Vol. II)

McGrath, Anne, with J. Treffs. *Wildflowers of the Adirondacks.* North Country Books, Sylvan Beach, N.Y., 1981

Murie, Olaus J. *A Field Guide to Animal Tracks.* Houghton Mifflin Company, Boston, 1954

Newcomb, Lawrence. *Newcomb's Wildflower Guide.* Little, Brown and Company, Boston, 1977

Ogden, Eugene C. *Field Guide to Northeastern Ferns.* New York State Museum. Bulletin Number 44, 1981

Peterson, Roger Tory. *A Field Guide to the Birds.* Houghton Mifflin Company, Boston, 1980

Peterson, Roger Tory and M. McKenny. *A Field Guide to Wildflowers of Northeastern and North-central North America.* Houghton Mifflin Company, Boston, 1968

Petrides, George A. *A Field Guide to Trees and Shrubs.* Houghton Mifflin Company, Boston, 1972

Phelps, Orra A. "Mountaintop Flora," in *The Adirondack High Peaks and the Forty-Sixers.* Pp. 277–290. The Peters Print, Albany, 1970

Smith, Clyde H. *The Adirondacks.* The Viking Press, New York, 1976

VanDiver, Bradford B. *Rocks and Routes of the North Country.* Humphrey, Geneva, New York, 1976

Wyckoff, Jerome. *The Adirondack Landscape: A Hiker's Guide.* Adirondack Mountain Club, Glens Falls, New York, 1967

Glossary

AEROBIC   Requiring molecular oxygen or air to live. Also, an area or zone in which such oxygen is available.

CANOPY   The upper layer or stratum of a community; the surface that first intercepts sunlight from above. Forests are commonly subdivided into five semi-distinct strata, including the tree layer, shrub layer, herbaceous layer, ground-cover and soil stratum. Trees normally occupy the canopy of a forest, but herbs and grasses may constitute the canopy of pastureland.

CIRQUE   A steep-walled amphitheater or basin, scoured by the plucking action of a glacier at a valley head.

CLIMAX COMMUNITY   The kind of community capable of perpetuating itself indefinitely on a particular site under the prevailing climatic and soil conditions. Climax communities are characterized by relative stability and are said to be at equilibrium with their environment. Many hundreds of years may be required for them to develop from a succession of less stable, preclimax communities.

COMMUNITY   The living part of an ecosystem; an assemblage of plants, animals, bacteria and fungi that live in the same environment and interact with one another. Examples include northern hardwood forest, mixed-wood forest, bog, pond, and alpine communities.

CONIFER   A cone-bearing tree having needles or scale-like foliage such as pine, spruce, hemlock, fir, larch and cedar. See also EVERGREEN.

CRUSTACEAN   A member of a large group of chiefly aquatic arthropods, including the shrimps, water fleas, fish lice, aquatic sow bugs, crayfish, and others commonly covered with a soft shell of chitin.

DECIDUOUS   Shedding leaves at a certain season.

DECOMPOSERS   Organisms of decay, usually bacteria and fungi, that break down dead organic material into simpler compounds and elements. Products of decomposition form the pool of nutrients that are used to sustain other plants and animals.

DRIFT   Any material, including till and outwash, deposited by glacial processes.

DUFF   The matted, partly decomposed organic surface layer of forest soils.

ECOLOGY   The study of the interrelationships between living things and their environment. It is the modern equivalent of natural history or field biology and is a multidisciplinary science that incorporates aspects of such diverse fields as botany, zoology, meterology, chemistry, soil science, and taxonomy.

ECOSYSTEM   A community and its environment treated together, including all the interactions of its members. Thus a conifer-dominated forest atop an esker of infertile, well-drained gravel and sand is an ecosystem, as is the plankton community of a pond when treated with its aquatic environment.

ENVIRONMENT   All the external conditions, such as soil, water, air, light, temperature, and organisms surrounding a living thing. Small, localized differences in such factors are often distinguished by the prefix "micro," as in microenvironment, microclimate, or microhabitat, depending upon which factors are considered.

ESKER   A long, narrow ridge of sand and gravel deposited by a glacial stream in an ice tunnel. In the Adirondacks, eskers range up to about 100 feet in height and often wind over the landscape for several miles.

EVEN-AGED   A forest stand composed of trees or other vegetation having no, or relatively small, differences in age.

EVERGREEN   Any plant remaining green throughout the year. Commonly used as synonymous with "conifer," but larch is a conifer that loses its needles each year and many plants, such as laurel and wintergreen, are evergreens but not conifers.

EXTIRPATE   To eradicate from a particular region. Not to be confused with extinction, which denotes complete annihilation or loss of a species. The timber wolf, cougar, moose, bald eagle and peregrine falcon have been extirpated from the Adirondacks, although stray individuals of certain of these species may at times be seen here.

HABITAT   The kind of environment where an organism lives; the immediate surroundings, living and nonliving, of an organism. Sugar maple grows in the deep, fertile, well-drained glacial till soils of lower mountain slopes; the spruce grouse inhabits coniferous lowlands associated with spruce swamps and bogs.

HARDPAN   A hardened soil layer caused by cementation of soil particles with organic matter or other compounds.

HARDWOOD   In common usage, any broad-leaved deciduous tree, as distinguished from a coniferous tree.

HEATH   A relatively open, level area characterized by a community of plants belonging to the heath family, such as blueberries, cranberries, laurel, leatherleaf, and other species common in bogs and on infertile sandy soils.

HERBACEOUS   Plants such as wildflowers having a fleshy (not woody) stem that normally dies back to the ground after each growing season.

HERBIVORE   A plant eater.

HUMUS   That portion of the soil organic matter remaining after the major portion of animal and plant residues have decomposed. Usually it is dark colored.

INDICATOR SPECIES   Any organism whose presence in a certain location is a fairly certain sign that particular environmental conditions are also present. For example, the presence of cattails normally indicates flooding of the soil surface during at least a portion of every growing season.

KAME   A more or less conical hill, usually of gravel or sand, deposited in a depression along the ice front or in a crack or hole within the ice border of a glacier.

KETTLE   A bowl-like depression or pit in glacial outwash, ranging up to about 25 feet deep and from a few tens of feet to over a mile in diameter. Kettles are formed when isolated blocks of glacial ice are covered with sand and gravel that slumps downward following melting of the ice. Water-filled kettles are called kettle ponds.

LIVERWORTS   Small, green mosslike plants having flattened bodies and lacking true stems, roots or leaves.

MESIC   Environmental conditions that have medium moisture supplies rather than hygric (wet) or xeric (dry) conditions.

METAMORPHIC ROCK   Rock that has been changed from its original form under conditions of intense heat, pressure, and possibly the introduction of new chemical substances.

MICROCLIMATE   See ENVIRONMENT.

MINERAL SOIL   A soil consisting predominantly of inorganic (mineral) material; usually containing less than about 20% organic matter.

MOLLUSK   A member of a large group of shellfish, including the slugs, snails, clams, mussels and others commonly covered with a hard calcareous shell.

NURSE CROP   Any vegetation that overtops lower, sometimes younger or slower-growing vegetation and in so doing fosters the lower plants by providing a certain amount of protection from sun, wind, rain, and temperature extremes.

OLD-GROWTH FOREST   Natural forest virtually uninfluenced by human activity; most often used in reference to a stand dominated by trees that are more than about 200 years old. An old-growth forest may be part of a climax community but is not necessarily so.

ORGANIC MATTER   Material that is living or is derived from living things. Common organic materials in soil include leaves, bark, needles, roots, bacteria, fungi, insects, worms and waste products of such life forms.

OUTWASH   A water-laid deposit of glacial drift that has been sorted into layers of relatively homogeneous material, primarily consisting of sand and gravel.

OXBOW   A bend in a river or stream shaped so that only a neck of land is left between two parts of the waterway. As waterways meander, they often create oxbows that may later be cut off from the main stream and be left as a pond, lake, or high-water flood basin.

PIONEER SPECIES   Any organism adapted to environmental conditions associated with site disturbance and typically forming part of a relatively simple community of sun-lovers. Pioneers normally modify their environment to such an extent that they are gradually replaced by species better adapted to the new conditions.

PLANKTON   Microscopic, nearly invisible organisms that are suspended in water and carried passively by currents. The plankton community consists of green plants (phytoplankton), animals (zooplankton) feeding on them, and predatory animals feeding on other animals, bacteria, and fungi.

PLEISTOCENE   A geologic epoch, lasting from about 1-1/2 million years ago to 10,000 years ago, during which time much of North America, northern Europe and northern Asia were covered by glacial ice.

RESPIRATION   The process whereby large, energy-rich molecules of food are broken down chemically and energy is released. It is a process that must occur in every living thing.

RIFFLE   A fast-water section of a stream where the shallow water races over stones and gravel.

SEDIMENTARY ROCK   Rock formed from deposits of sediment within water. Sedimentary rocks are usually layered (stratified).

SITE   An area considered in terms of its physical environment. Normally used to denote the potential of an area to produce a certain type of community, now or at some future date. Thus, a northern hardwood site can be expected to foster the development of a northern hardwood community, whereas a site on moist outwash sands would probably support a mixed-wood community.

STAND   An aggregation of trees or other growth occupying a specific area and sufficiently uniform in composition, age arrangement, and condition as to be distinguishable from the forest or other growth on adjoining areas.

TILL   An unstratified deposit of glacial drift consisting of a relatively heterogeneous mixture of clay, sand, silt, gravel and boulders.

UNDERSTORY   The layer of a community that lies between the upper surface or canopy and the ground, normally occupied by trees and shrubs in a forest. See CANOPY.

VIRGIN FOREST   See OLD-GROWTH FOREST.

WETLAND   Any land where saturation with water is the dominant factor determining the nature of soil development and the types of plant-and-animal communities living in the soil and on its surface. The single feature that most wetlands share is soil or substrate that is at least periodically saturated with or covered by water. Wetlands are commonly referred to as a bog, swamp or marsh.

Index

Text references in roman,
illustration references in *italic*.

abandoned field community, *40*, 41–44
Adirondack Forest Preserve, 16
Adirondack Park, formation of, 16
   map, *10*
Adirondack Park Agency, 16
alder, mountain, 120
   speckled, *68, 69*
Algonquin Peak, *116*
   view from, *20*
   alpine meadow, *112*
Algonquins, 15
alpine community, 113–123
arrowhead, 73, *76*
ash, black, 69
   white, 44, 54
ash, mountain-, *105*, 106
aspen(s), *40*, 41, 44, 47, 97
   bigtooth, 44
   quaking (trembling), 44, *45*, 49
aster(s), 41
   New England, *42*
Ausable River, West Branch, *91*

bacteria, 78, 97
Barkeaters, 15
bass, 97
basswood, 54
Bazzania, three-lobed, 107
bear, black, 47, *50*, 51, 98
beaver, 73, 97–98, *100*
   pond, *101*
beech, American, 47, *49, 50*, 51, *52, 53*, 61, 103

beech bark disease, 51
bellwort, 53
bilberry, alpine, *117, 120, 121*
birch, dwarf, 120
   mountain paper, *106*, 120
   paper (white), *34*, 44, 47, 49, 106
   yellow, 44, *49*, 51, 61, 103
bittern, American, *76*
blackbird(s), 39
   red-wing, 39, 73
   rusty, 82
blackberry, *45*
black-fly larvae, 90
blowdown, 33, 35, 45–47, 59, 69, 111
blueberries, *46*, 47, 62, *63*
bluebird, 41
bobolink, *38*
bogs, 33, 67, *77,* 77–86, *85*
boreal forest, 33, *102*, 103–111, *105, 106, 107, 109*
briars, *45,* 47
buckbean, 78
bunchberry, 62, *63*, 107, 120
bunting, indigo, 41
burns, 45–47, *46, 106* (See also fires.)
bur-reed, 73
butternut, 54
buttonbush, 69

caddisflies, 90
Cascade Mountain, *8, 18*
catbird, 47
cattails, *72, 73*

cedar, northern white-, 69, 103
    red-, eastern, *40* 41
Chapel Pond, *34*
Champlain, Samuel de, 16
cherry, black, 61
    pin, 44, *45,* 47
chestnut, American, 54
chickadee, boreal, 70, *108*
    black-capped, *64*
chicory, 39, *43*
chipmunk, *53,* 54
cinquefoil, three-toothed, *119*
cirque, glacial, 25, *105*
clear-cutting, 16, 45
climax communities, 33, 103
clubmoss, bristly, 120
    shining, *52, 53*
Colden, Mt., *20*
coontails, 73
cottongrass, *81*
cowbird, brown-headed, 39
coyote, *40,* 44, 76, 98
cranberry, 79
crickets, 41
crossbill, red-winged, *65,* 70
    white-winged, 70
crow, *39*
crowberry, black, *120*
Crustaceans, 98

dace, blacknose, 92, *130*
daisy, 41
dandelion, 39
damselfly(s), 92
    spread-winged, *72*
darter, greenside, 92

deer's hair, *112, 117,* 118, *121*
deer, white-tailed, *44,* 47, 54, 69
Diapensia, *114,* 118, *121*
disturbed areas, as sites for natural communities, 33, 35, 37–47
    (See also blowdown, fires, burns, logging, clear-cutting.)
dock, 73
dogwood(s), 40, 69
    red-panicle, 41
dogwood, dwarf (See bunchberry.)
dove, rock, 37
dragonfly, 92
drift, glacial, *24,* 26, 57
duck, wood, 70
duff, 107, 115

ecotone, 103
elderberry, 47
elm(s), 44, 54
    American, 70, *37*
Emmons, Ebenezer, 15–16
erratic, glacial, *26*
esker, glacial, 27–*29, 28,* 47, *59*
everlasting, pearly, 41

farmlands, as sites for natural communities, 37–41
fern(s), *26, 46, 52, 76, 107*
    bracken, 47, *46*
    marginal woodfern, *52*
    marsh, *76*
    polypody, *26*
    spinulose woodfern, 53, 62, *107*
finch, purple, 70
fir, balsam, 61, *63,* 69, 82, *102,* 103–*104, 106, 109, 111,* 120
fires, 16, 33, 35, 45–47, *46,* 59, 97, 106, 122

fish, 73, *88,* 98, *130* (See also bass, dace, minnow, trout.)
flycatcher, alder, 70
   olive-sided, 82
foamflower, *53,* 54
Forest Preserve, 16
fox(es), 76
   red, 44
frog(s), 82
   gray treefrog, *75,* 76
   green, 76
   mink, *79*
   spring peeper, *75,* 76
   wood, 73
fungi, 78, 97

Giant Mountain, 105
glacier(s), *22,* 23–29 (See also cirque, drift, erratic, esker, kame, kettle, outwash, till.)
goldenrod, 41, *43*
goldfinch, American, 41, *42*
goldthread, *63*
Gothics, *98–99*
grackle, 39
Grass River Flow, *66–67*
grass-pink, *5,* 79
grasshopper(s), 41
grosbeak, evening, *64,* 65
grouse, ruffed, 44, 47
   spruce, 82, *83*

hardpan, 59
hardwood forest, 33, *48,* 49–54
hare, snowshoe, *54,* 108
hare's tail, 120
harrier, northern, *72,* 82

hawk(s), 76
   broad-winged, 54
   red-tailed, 37
hawkweed, 39
hawthorn, 41
Haystack Mountain, *14*
heal-all, 39
hellebore, false, 120
hellgrammites, 92
hemlock, eastern, *51,* 53, 61, 82
heron(s), 73
   great blue, *72*
hickory, shagbark, 54
High Peaks, *36*
hobblebush, *52,* 53, *54, 55*
holly, mountain, *68,* 69
holygrass, alpine, 118
hophornbeam, eastern, 54
humus, 53, 106, 107
Hurricane Mountain, *102*

insects, 41, 65, 73, 79, 98
Iroquois, 15

Jack-in-the-pulpit, 54
jay, blue, 82
   gray, 82, *87*
junco, dark-eyed, 111, *118,* 122
juniper, pasture, *40,* 41

kame, glacial, 27–*29, 28,* 59
kestrel, American, 41, 82
kettle, glacial, 27–*29,* 95
killdeer, *38*
kinglet, golden-crowned, *64,* 65, 110
   ruby-crowned, *64,* 70

krummholz, *116,* 120–*122*

Labrador tea, 79, *81, 120*
Lake Placid, *32*
lake overturn, *96*
lake stratification, *96*
larch (tamarack), 33, 70, 77, *83, 84, 85, 86,* 103
laurel, bog, *81,* 120
  sheep, 62, *77, 81*
leatherleaf, *77, 79, 81,* 120
lemming, bog, 82
lichen(s), *32,* 63, 115, *121*
  old man's beard, *108*
lily, bluebead, *63, 107,* 120
liverworts, 53, 62, 107
logging, 16, *17,* 33, 35, 45–47, 97
loosestrife, 73

maple(s), 103
  mountain, *103*
  red, 44, 47, *57, 61, 63,* 69
  silver, 70
  striped, *52,* 53, *140*
  sugar, *49,* 50, 51
Marcy, Mt., 16
marshes, *66, 67, 72,* 73–76, 97
marten, pine (American sable), 108
mayflower, Canada, 62, *63*
mayfly, 90
meadow, wet, 73, 97
meadowlands (abandoned fields), as natural communities, *40,* 41–44
meadowlark, eastern, *38*
meadowsweet, 47
mergansers, *6*

mouse (mice), 37
  deer, 108
  meadow jumping, 41
milkweed, 41, *43*
mink, 76
minnow, fathead, 92
mixed woods, 33, *56,* 57–65
mollusks, 98
moss(es), *26, 52,* 53, 57, *62,* 107, 115, 120, *121*
  mountain fern, 107
  rock, 115
  sphagnum, 70, *71, 78, 81,* 84, *85,* 115, 118
  (See also peat.)
  stair-step, *53*
  water, 90
Mount Colden, *20*
mountain glacier, *22*
mountain-ash, *105,* 106
mullein, 41, *43*
muskrat, 73, 76
  push-up, *138*

nettle, stinging, 54
Noonmark Mountain, *105*
northern hardwood forest, 33, *48,* 49–54
nuthatch, red-breasted, *64*

oak, red, 54
  white, 54
open water (lakes and ponds), as a natural community, 89, 92–98
orchis, white-fringed, 79, *126*
osprey, 73
outwash, glacial, 26–29, *27,* 33, 47, 50, 51, 57, 67, 95
ovenbird, 54
overturn, 95, *96*
owl, 76

peat, 78, 79, 82, 84, 86
Pharoah Lake, *125*
pickerelweed, *72,* 73
pine(s), 82
    pitch, 47, 61
    red, *60, 61, 65*
    white, *40,* 41, *46,* 47, 57, *58, 59, 60, 61*
pioneer species, 33, 44, 49, 51, 106, 115
pitcher plant, *78,* 79
plankton, 73, 95, 97
pondweeds, 73
pools and riffles, as sites for natural communities, 90–92, *91, 93*
porcupine, 39

rabbit, 39
raccoon, 39
raisin, wild, 69, *70*
raspberry, 47
raven, common, *123*
redcedar, eastern, *40,* 41
reeds, 73
rivers and streams, as natural communities, 89–*91, 93,* 95
rosebay, Lapland, *114,* 118
rosemary, bog, *77,* 79, *81*
rushes, 73

St. Johnsworts, 41, *42*
St. Regis Canoe Area, *94*
sable, American (pine marten), 108
sandwort, mountain, 118, *119*
sarsaparilla, wild, 53
Sawteeth, *98–99*
sedge(s), 73, *76*
    Bigelow, 118
shiner, rosyface, 92

shrew, masked, 108
    short-tailed, 41
siskin, pine, *64, 65*
skunk, 39
smartweed, 73
snails, 73
snakes, 37
sorrel, sheep, *46,* 47
    wood, 62, *107*
sparrow, Lincoln's, 82
    song, *45,* 47
    swamp, 70
    vesper, 41
    white-throated, *110,* 122–123, *134*
spruce(s), 61, 82, 103, 106
    black, 69, *77, 84, 85,* 111, 120
    red, 53, 61, *102,* 103–*104, 106, 111*
spruce flat, 70
spruce slope community, *102,* 108–111
spruce swamp, *71*
squirrel, red, 65, 108
starflower, *63*
Stoddard, Seneca Ray, "Lumbering in the Adirondacks," *17*
sumac, staghorn, 41
sundew, round-leaved, 79
swamp(s), 67, *69*–70, 97
    conifer, 70, *71*
    deciduous wooded, 70
    shrub, *69*
    wooded, 69–70
sweetgale, 69, *70*
swift, chimney, 47

tamarack (larch), 33, 70, *77, 83, 84, 85, 86,* 103
tanager, scarlet, 54
teasel, 41
thistle, bull, *42*

thrush, gray-cheeked, 110
    northern water, 70
    Swainson's, 110
till, glacial, 26–27, 33, 49, 51, 95
toad, American, *75*
treeline, *111*
trout, 97
    native brook (speckled), *88,* 92
twinflower, *63,* 120

uplift, geological, 21
Upper Ausable Lake, *98–99*

vervain, 73
violet, Canada, 54
vireo, red-eyed, 54
vole, red-backed, 47
vulture, turkey, 39, *45*

warbler, blackpoll, 110
    Canada, 70
    chestnut-sided, 47
    magnolia, 70
    yellow, 47
    yellow-rumped, 110
water boatmen, 92
water pennies, *90*
water striders, 92
waterlilies, 73, *74*
waterweeds, 73
wetlands, 33, 67–86, 95
Whiteface Mountain, *32*
willow(s), 69
    bearberry, *114, 118,* 120
winter kill, 96
winterberry, *68,* 69

wintergreen, 62
woodchuck, *37*
woodcock, American, 70
woodpecker, black-backed, *82*
    downy, *64*
    three-toed, 82

yellowthroat, common, 76

zooplankton (See plankton.)

Notes

A fawn lies hidden in a forest glade.